Dr. R. A. FORREST (about whom this book is written) and the Toccoa Falls Institute are, in a sense, synonymous. He it was who breathed into the school the breath of life; he has been its mainstay throughout its forty-five years of existence; and he is still exerting a guiding and steadying influence in shaping its destiny.

For those of you who may first become acquainted with this Christian school through the pages of this book, the following brief resume is presented.

THE TOCCOA FALLS INSTITUTE was begun in 1911 to offer educational opportunity to young people who perhaps became Christians after reaching maturity and who desired training to fit them to become Christian workers. Today the school has a four-year high school course, a vocational course, a commercial department, and a four-year Bible course — offering the degree Bachelor of Arts in Biblical Education. The Institute helps to develop the character and intellect of hundreds who come from all parts of the United States and other countries, enabling them to become good citizens and fruitful servants for the Lord around the world. The sun never sets on the work of former students and graduates of Toccoa Falls.

DR. R. A. FORREST, President

Achieving the Impossible
... with God

The Life Story of Dr. R. A. Forrest

by

LORENE MOOTHART, A.B., M.A.

Director of Speech Department,
Toccoa Falls Institute

✠

43987

Publishing Agents

CHRISTIAN PUBLICATIONS, INC.

Third & Reily Sts., Harrisburg, Pa.

(Printed in U. S. A.)

Dedication

This book is dedicated to Mrs. R. A. Forrest, whose consecrated character and undying love have been of inestimable value to her husband; whose valiant spirit and assistance have helped make possible the Toccoa Falls Institute; and whose influence upon the students is one of the sweetest memories they carry from the school.

Foreword

EVERY DAY we live we understand better the words of Alexander Pope, "The proper study of mankind is man." However fascinating the natural sciences may be, that which wins the interest of the greatest number of intelligent persons and holds it for the longest time is the study of other persons. Rocks and trees and stars cannot love and breathe and smile and suffer and rejoice. Only people can do these things. While our minds may enjoy finding out about stars and trees and rocks, our hearts search for something that can respond to their outgoing affection, and only people can do that perfectly. Hence the universal popularity of biography.

In short it is the *warmth* in human beings that other human beings enjoy; and there is hardly another word that would better describe the subject of this book, Dr. R. A. Forrest. His is a warm personality. His preaching is warm, his heart is warm, his whole relation to others is sympathetic, affectionate and congenial. This fact, more than anything else explains why he is loved by so many people. "He that would have friends must show himself friendly."

In at least two fields of Christian endeavor R. A. Forrest has excelled, that of the Christian ministry and Christian education. But however well his preaching has been received by the thousands who have heard him over the years, it is my opinion that in the time to come he will be remembered chiefly for his consecrated work among Christian youth. To study under a man of the fervent spirituality of R. A. Forrest is a high privilege for any young man or woman. And all over the world there are those who have had that privilege and who will and do rise up to call him blessed who foresaw their needs and founded an institution to meet those needs long before they themselves were aware of how needy they were.

Dr. Forrest began on the proverbial shoestring and all that he has accomplished is by prayer and faith and hard work. Yet there is about him nothing of the martyr. After hearing about his struggles, his trials, his victories in prayer, one would expect to find a man lean and ascetic looking who rarely smiled and who took himself very seriously indeed. Imagine the surprise to find him a round-faced, almost jolly man who can laugh till the windows vibrate and whose whole bearing is relaxed and completely good humored. And when he tells something of his early trials one gets the sly impression that he enjoyed his troubles. And if the whole truth be told, I think he did.

Much might be said about this man, but I think that the most significant thing that may be said is that he lived so as to make God necessary to him. Extract God from R. A. Forrest and you have exactly nothing left. He wanted it that way. And that is perhaps the one great lesson his life teaches. "Not I, but Christ liveth in me." That is the real secret of his life. And a life like that is bound to be a success.

A. W. Tozer.

Preface

DR. FORREST has been asked many, many times to put into a book his experiences in evangelistic work and in establishing and maintaining the Toccoa Falls Institute. A humble man of God, he has been reluctant to do so; only recently has his permission to write such a book been obtained.

This book is offered as a record of the faithfulness of God in answering the prayers of His loyal servant. It contains many of the stories used widely by Dr. Forrest to illustrate his sermons. His actual wording is retained insofar as possible. These stories are woven together historically—beginning with his boyhood, continuing with his early preparation and training, recounting the early days of the Institute, showing some of the results obtained by him as both evangelist and educator, and bringing up-to-date the record of the work of the school which he founded. The many miracles wrought by God in answer to the prayers of His consecrated servant cannot but astound the average man.

Perhaps Dr. Forrest's life can best be summarized in the words of Psalm 71, verses 17 and 18: *O God, thou hast taught me from my youth: and hitherto have I declared thy wondrous works. Now also when I am old and grey-headed, O God, forsake me not; until I have shewed thy strength unto this generation, and thy power to every one that is to come.*

Chapter One

"Your young men shall see visions."—JOEL 2:28

THEY STOOD on the veranda of Haddock Inn, the two of them, overlooking a sparkling lake. In the quiet of the afternoon they could hear, at a short distance, the splashing of the waters of Toccoa Creek as they leapt and fell one hundred eighty-six feet to form the beautiful Toccoa Falls, so named by the Cherokee Indians. The wooded mountains of northeast Georgia formed a magnificent backdrop for the hotel—and for the transaction that would soon be consummated, a transaction that must have been heralded in Glory, a transaction that has led to the spread of the Gospel in many parts of the earth and the winning of many precious souls to the Lord.

The older man looked at the younger, sizing him up. Yes, this Richard Forrest looked as though he'd measure up to expectations. True, those were mighty glowing terms that D. J. Fant, Christian engineer on the Southern Railroad, had used in speaking of this young man. A man would have to be unusual to be able to live up to such a description. Well, he'd reserve his opinion for a bit. Wait and see what the young fellow'd say. He'd shown him the place. Mighty good looking piece of property, if he did say so himself.

Good looking piece of property? As Richard Forrest looked it over, he felt it truly more than an answer to prayer. It was all that D. J. Fant had said—and more. Haddock Inn, a popular summer resort, containing fifty-eight rooms, most of them fifteen feet square, all furnished; a 750-foot veranda, upon which they now stood in the late afternoon; modern plumbing, bathrooms with hot and cold water; electric lights! What an ideal set-up for a Christian school! Since Haddock Inn had been a summer resort, there would be the need for better heating facilities during the winter months, but that could be remedied. "Surely God has answered our prayers and directed me here," thought Richard Forrest. "Why, the arrangement is so nearly ideal that it looks as though the builder of the Inn had in mind using it for a Christian school." Indeed, such was the case.

But reality must be faced and the reality was that while this was the property to which he felt the Lord had directed him, yet Richard Forrest had only $10.00 in his pocket—and no where to get more. No where but from his Heavenly Father.

So he, in turn, stole a surreptitious look at the man by whose side he stood. He was a business man in Toccoa, in fact, the owner of the bank. He'd want money, a sizable down payment, and good terms. And he had a right to ask it. Business was business, and you couldn't run it on sentiment. This was a valuable piece of property. Dared he even ask the price? But *He giveth power to the faint,* so Richard Forrest breathed a silent prayer, wet his lips, and stammered out the question: "How much do you want for the hotel?"

The owner looked out over the lake, then back to the young man standing by his side. "Twenty-five thousand dollars is a fair price, it seems to me. That will include not only the hotel but also about one hundred acres surrounding it."

"Will Toccoa Falls be on that hundred acres?"

"Yes, sir. There's a little piece of land that won't be included, though. My power plant is built there, and I'll retain that small piece of property and the water rights to Toccoa Creek above the Falls."

"Fair enough, sir," replied Mr. Forrest. "But tell me, what about our lights here?"

"Oh, we'll furnish you light with no obligations as long as there's water to turn the generator."

"I surely appreciate your kindness, sir. And the price is certainly reasonable. Only . . . "

"Only what?" barked the older man.

"It's about the terms, sir." Mr. Forrest reached into his pocket and fingered his ten dollar bill.

"What about the terms? I haven't even mentioned them yet."

"I know—but I have only ten dollars, and no tangible place to get any more."

As the business man drew in his breath and opened his mouth, the youthful Forrest watched, fascinated yet fearful. Now would come the refusal—but he must have this place! This was God's place for him, he knew. Suddenly the words were tumbling out.

"Sir, I know this must sound presumptuous to you, a business man and a banker. But I *know* God wants us to establish a school for Him here. Sir, I'll pay you ten dollars (I have only that and my return ticket to Atlanta), and the Lord and I will owe you the other $24,990.00 on the $25,000.00 deal if you'll trust the Lord and us."

Now it was said. It was an overbold proposition, he knew. Yet it was the only one he could offer. Practically holding his breath, he waited for the answer.

"I can trust the Lord," was the dry response. The business man held out his hand for the ten dollar bill.

Such was the beginning of an institution in northeast Georgia, a Bible school that started with one building situated on one hundred acres of land and that has grown to sixty-three buildings on nearly eleven hundred acres, a school whose influence has been felt not only nearby but to the ends of the earth. Surely God put His seal of approval on the transaction carried out that day, January 1, 1911.

Chapter Two

"And ye shall seek me, and find me, when you shall search for me with all your heart."—JEREMIAH 29:13

RICHARD ALEXANDER FORREST, one of four children, was born into a modest—yes, even poor—home in the outskirts of Wilmington, Delaware, on July 14, 1881. His father, a factory worker, was a man feared by his family during Richard's boyhood. (After his conversion during middle life, he became entirely changed, a fine and noble Christian man.) His mother was a woman of high ideals, a church-going woman—living as best she knew how and bringing up her children with high ideals. She constantly encouraged her boy in his efforts to educate himself to serve the Lord and instilled into his heart Christian principles that have guided him throughout his life.

In his paternal grandmother's home Richard learned the stern discipline, adherence to principle, and rigorous religious training of his Scottish ancestors. To his Scotch Presbyterian grandmother he recited the Shorter Catechism at the age of ten. Grandmother never cooked on Sunday, except for making her cup of hot tea. She never allowed newspapers in the house on Sunday; and when the Forrest children came to visit her on the Lord's Day, as they often did, they read good books. Although they felt that Sunday was a bore at Grandmother's house, they loved to listen to her Scotch brogue as she told them Bible stories.

Richard's other grandmother was Irish, and she spent her last years in the Forrest home. From her Richard heard, and never forgot, a graphic illustration of God's will. Richard had just come home from the funeral of a neighbor boy several years older than he. His grandmother called him to her rocker and asked him to sit down. "I want to tell you a story," said she, "and I don't want you to forget it." This is the story she told:

"A number of years ago a child was born to a young couple. They loved this baby boy dearly; in fact, the mother almost worshiped him. But when the child was still a baby, he grew very ill. In spite of all the doctor could do, the fever continued to mount until he despaired of the baby's life. A Christian man, he called the young mother to him and said, 'I think God wants your baby.'

"'What do you mean?' the mother screamed. 'Do you mean my baby's going to die? I won't let him die! God can't have my baby!'

"'Now, now,' the doctor reasoned, 'you should be very careful what you say. God knows better than we do. If it's His will that your baby die—well, God's will should be done.'

"The woman turned blazing eyes to him, then looked down at the still form of her babe. Already the child seemed to be gasping his last breath. Suddenly she grabbed her baby out of his crib, held him up toward heaven, and shook him violently as she defied God: 'You can't have my baby! I won't let You have him! He's mine! He's mine! He *will* stay alive! I'm going to keep him!'

"Again she shook the child violently. Later the doctor said he didn't know whether it was the furious shaking or what, but the baby began to breathe again, and from that moment was on the road to recovery.

"Richard, you have just come home from that boy's funeral. He has always been an outlaw. He has broken his mother's heart again and again. He was hanged for murder on his twenty-first birthday!"

As a boy, Richard was encouraged to join a boy's club, somewhat similar to the Boy Scouts of today. A Christian woman, neighbor to the Forrests, sponsored this group of boys and endeavored to help them toward the building of a better life. It was through this neighbor that Richard first received the vision of a larger life than that of the others living around him. He didn't know how to gain it, but he felt vaguely that there must be something more to living than he yet knew.

A little later, still unsaved, he felt the urge to become a Christian worker of some kind, hardly daring to hope that some day he might be a minister.

While Richard was having these disquieting feelings and uncertain desires, he was quite startled by a statement made by his mother. One Sunday morning as the family was walking home from church, Mrs. Forrest remarked to a neighbor: "I think Richard is going to be a minister." He felt an uncanny sensation, and never forgot those words. Surely God must have indicated to Mrs. Forrest that His hand was on her eldest son.

The lad, now sixteen, began to search more diligently for an answer to these inner cravings for a better, fuller life. And God began to answer, for a godly Sunday-school teacher, Miss Margaret Rogers, a woman who loved boys and was concerned about their souls, gathered together a group of teen-age fellows, of whom Richard was one. Earnestly she labored, diligently she taught, striving to lead "her boys" to Christ.

One night Richard, who by this time was seventeen, attended a cottage prayer meeting held in Miss Rogers' home. It was at this meeting that he made the most momentous decision of his life; for it was on this occasion that he met his Lord and accepted Him as his Saviour. Now the vague longings and desires were crystallized; now his life had focus. Now he knew the meaning, the embodiment, of the larger life. Now he had new zeal and devotion. Never once since has he lost sight of what God meant for him to do with his life.

Soon afterward he united with the Rodney Street Presbyterian Church of Wilmington, during the ministry of the Rev. William McCorkle, D.D.

When Richard made his decision to become a Christian, he felt no particular emotion—just a quiet conviction that Christ had shed His precious blood for Richard's sins, too, and that he should acknowledge Him as Saviour and Lord of his life. However, the Holy Spirit put His definite seal of approval on the transaction later that same evening.

It was 10:30 p.m. Richard was on his way home from the cottage prayer meeting at which he had been converted. He was alone—there was nothing humorous about that. He was walking past a Roman Catholic convent—nothing funny about that, either. But suddenly he was seized with a spirit of laughter—he laughed himself into hysterics on the way home. And he's been laughing or chuckling ever since. It has been, in a sense, his trademark.

Now this would not seem unusual, unless you had known Richard's nature before he became a Christian. It seems almost impossible to believe, but he was a natural born grouch. He never smiled. For three or four days at a time he would not even speak to any member of the family. His mother used to apologize to company for Richard's grumpiness.

So it was, that when he was born into the kingdom of God, he was given a new disposition—the spirit of laughter. Thousands upon thousands have been encouraged and lives have been saved by his little chuckle or hearty laugh.

Chapter Three

"And he left all, rose up, and followed him."—LUKE 5:28

DURING HIS BOYHOOD, Richard Forrest had chosen engineering as his profession. His father had often mentioned the fact that the chief engineer at the factory in which he worked made the then fabulous sum of ten dollars a day. Two hundred and fifty dollars a month, thought Richard, that's for me! For a time after his conversion and even after the consecration of his life to the Lord, he still felt drawn to engineering as his life's work.

To this end, having completed the course of study in the grade and high schools of Wilmington, he decided to enter college. To be sure, there was no money to go away from home, but there was an Extension Division of Delaware College in Wilmington; so he enrolled there. However, the Lord was speaking to him. Before long he determined that, as soon as the present term ended, he should give up the idea of an engineering career and instead go to some kind of school which would train him for Christian service.

At this time the Forrest home had an unusual visitor. One day the peace of the street was shattered by the arrival of the carriage of Mr. William Bancroft. Since Mr. Bancroft was the owner of the large factory at which Richard's father and many of the other men on the street worked, everyone knew his carriage. There was a great deal of rushing to doors, peering through window curtains, and speculating as to what Mr. Bancroft was doing on this humble street. Imagine the excitement when the coachman drove up in front of the Forrest home and came to a flourishing stop! What did Mr. William Bancroft want of the Forrests?

The coachman stepped down, opened the door of the carriage, and assisted Mr. Bancroft, a Quaker with flaming red whiskers, to alight. Seemingly unaware of the excitement he was arousing, Mr. Bancroft stalked up to the Forrest front door. By this time Richard's mother was at the door, wiping her hands on her apron, shoving a chair into line, pushing back a stray lock of hair, and wondering fearfully at the cause of the visit. Was her husband injured —maybe killed—at the plant? It must be some kind of disaster that would call for the personal visit of a man so powerful.

Mr. Bancroft interrupted her thoughts with, "I came to see thy boy."

Her boy? What had Richard done?—for she knew it must be he.

"Just a minute, sir. I'll call him." She rushed to his room, where even now he was studying.

"Richard, Richard, come quickly. Mr. Bancroft is here and wants to see you."

As the lad rose from his books and started to the door, his mother tried to pull him together. She tugged at his shirt and brushed at his hair, endeavoring to make him more presentable. "Richard, do you know what he wants?" But by this time they were in the presence of the august man.

"I understand thee is going to school to be a preacher," were Mr. Bancroft's opening words. Richard answered this in the affirmative.

"I want to tell thee it's a long hard road." Mr. Bancroft spent some time telling Richard the problems he'd face, the difficulties he'd undergo, the handicaps he'd have, the hurdles he'd have to jump. Not one word was said about money, nor did Mr. Bancroft ever offer to help the boy financially, but as he rose to leave, he said: "I shall think of thee and I shall pray for thee."

Probably his prayers and thoughts for the boy helped him face the future with God's particular guidance.

When Mr. Bancroft commended Mr. Forrest on his son's choice of the ministry as a profession, Mr. Forrest's comment was that it wasn't his idea for his boy to become a preacher. His ambition for Richard was that he might continue his course in engineering, and he was bitterly opposed to his son's becoming a minister.

For a time Richard endeavored to pursue his new course in life without causing a break with his father. Finally, he realized that an open break must come and that it couldn't be put off longer.

It was a hot Sunday afternoon. Richard's father was sitting near an open window, reading a newspaper. Richard had decided to join two of his friends in running a tent meeting sixteen miles away in New Castle, Delaware. His mother had already packed his telescope (an old-fashioned traveling bag). Nothing remained to be done—except to inform his father as to what he intended to do.

The youth stood, summoning what courage he could. He fidgeted, trying to determine how best he could word his farewell. He looked at his father, but the newspaper covered his face.

Finally Richard spoke to the open newspaper: "Pop, I'm going to help some boys in a tent meeting at New Castle."

The newspaper didn't move or rustle even slightly. But the words from behind that paper were quietly ominous.

"If you're going to a tent meeting, keep going. Don't come back."

Richard picked up the telescope and walked out. Over and over came those words on the way to New Castle.

After the service that evening came the problem of bunking. The other two fellows, Samuel McBride and Frank Hammel, slept in the tent. There were only two cots, and by right of priority these two occupied them. Richard slept on the platform.

That first night he didn't sleep very much. He kept hearing his father's words: "If you're going to a tent meeting, keep going—keep going—keep going." The platform got harder and harder. He thought of his comfortable bed at home, only a few miles away. For the first time, he really began to understand what Mr. Bancroft had been trying to tell him; he began to sense the price he'd have to pay if he followed the leading of his convictions. He courageously decided that it was worth the cost. He'd go on with the Lord.

Chapter Four

DURING THE SUMMER the three youths moved their tent
to Wilmington and began services there. As Richard walked
into the tent one day, he noticed a young lady at one side
taking books out of a trunk and placing them on a table
there. His natural curiosity, plus the attention the young
lady was receiving from the other fellows, made him hasten
over to become acquainted. Then she turned around! His
heart turned over! This was the girl of his dreams—the
girl whose loveliness he'd held enshrined in his heart for a
solid year.

It had been perhaps chance—no, it must have been the
leading of the Lord—that had brought him, a year before,
to a cottage prayer meeting on Jackson Street in Wilmington. As the group were assembling, three young ladies
came in and were introduced. "Come," said the hostess,
"I want you all to meet a young lady who has endeared
herself to us. She's a great worker for the Lord and is
planning to attend The Missionary Training Institute at
Nyack, New York, this fall. Thereupon she introduced
Miss Evelyn Drennen.

Miss Drennen was standing between the two other young
ladies, who were also introduced to the group. But for
Richard Forrest the faces of the other two faded into the
background. The room swirled; everything grew black
except the face of Miss Drennen, which was all he could
see, and he felt then that he wanted to look at that face
the rest of his life.

The meeting was called to order. Richard, coming somewhat out of his daze, made his way to a seat. However, he didn't know whether the group was singing "Yankee Doodle" or "Nearer, My God, to Thee." He couldn't have told whether the leader was reading the Scriptures or Sanskrit. All he could see or think of was that beautiful face and the fact that he must somehow become acquainted with Miss Drennen. "Evelyn, isn't that a beautiful name," he mused. "How musical! Eve-lyn, not Ev-lyn, as so many say. Eve-lyn! Eve-lyn! Eve-lyn!"

During the following year, he wrote one letter to this lovely girl at Nyack. Laboriously he penned that epistle, scarcely expecting her even to read it, hoping for—yet not anticipating—an answer. When she did send a reply, he actually and literally wore the letter out. He held her in such high reverence, though, that he didn't dare answer her letter—he just didn't dare write her again. He felt that she was so far above him that surely she wouldn't stoop so low as to continue a correspondence with him.

Now here she was, in person, in their tent! Joy unmingled flowed through him.

Richard Forrest was not the only one swept off his feet by this beautiful girl. Frank Hammel, another of the trio, was having similar thoughts. So it was that there were two anxious fellows a short time later when a note was sent down to the tent stating that Miss Drennen was very ill with asthma, and would they "send a man to fan her all night?"

Miss Drennen was living with an unmarried lady, Miss Mary Fisher, and her father. They could provide the necessary care for her, but the weather was extremely hot. Those were the days before electric fans; therefore, it became necessary to find someone who would be willing to sit by her bedside and fan her.

Frank, who was more or less the leader of the group,

grabbed the note, pocketed it, and ordered: "You fellows stay here and take care of things. I'll go offer my services for the care of Miss Drennen."

Richard rose. "Wait a minute, Frank. Did you notice the wording of that note? It said they wanted a *man* to fan Miss Drennen. I'm going!"

As the other fellows looked on with mouths agape, Richard turned on his heel and strode out.

You may be sure that the fanning did not stop once all through that night and that the labor seemed light, because it was a work of love.

Like Richard, Evelyn Drennen was trusting God for all her money. Her father wasn't able to help her, as their family was very poor, just like Richard's. However, unlike the Forrests, the Drennens had been prosperous. Evelyn's father had had a very productive farm, but had lost it in business reverses. After completing her schooling in the public schools of Cecil County, Maryland, Evelyn decided to prepare for a teaching career at the State Normal College at Newark, Delaware, and earned her way by doing housework in a private home there.

Now, feeling that God was directing her to full-time Christian service and realizing the need of training in a Bible institute, she was attending The Missionary Training Institute at Nyack, New York, during the winter months. In the summer, to help earn her way, Evelyn was selling books, literature, mottoes, and subscriptions to the "Christian Alliance." She had a trunk full of materials. Before each service she'd put her books and other items on display, and after the meeting put what hadn't been sold back into the trunk. Richard soon began helping her—and dared any other young fellow to put her books away for her at night or take them out of the trunk before services started. In that way they became more closely acquainted.

One night Richard gathered up his courage enough to

tell Evelyn how much he cared for her. Then, characteristically, they got down on their knees to pray about it. After they'd both prayed, to his intense amazement, she leaned over to kiss him—and he didn't know what she wanted! He backed away from her, he was so embarrassed. She was so far above him, he felt—he didn't think it possible that she'd stoop that low. He couldn't imagine—why, she was in a different world from him! So did he feel about the girl who was to become his wife and companion throughout more than half a century.

That night marked the beginning—not of sorrows—but of joys—for these two.

The following fall Evelyn Drennen resumed her studies at The Missionary Training Institute, where she became the target of much teasing by her roommate, Lillian Stemm, concerning her relationship to Richard. During a visit to Wilmington, Evelyn told Richard what her friends were saying. He asked her: "What did you say?"

She responded: "I told Lillian that you're my brother in Christ."

A bit irked, he replied, "What do you want to tell her that for? You know better than that. You know I'm more than that."

"Well," she retorted, spiritedly, "that's all I can say. You've never asked me to marry you."

Later Dr. Forrest was accustomed, when speaking of this occasion, to say, with a twinkle in his eye: "There wasn't anything else to do and still be a gentleman. So I asked her to marry me."

But don't think he didn't want to ask her! Or that he wasn't the happiest person in the world when she answered in the affirmative.

Chapter Five

"Get wisdom, get understanding: forget it not; neither decline from the words of my mouth."—PROVERBS 4:5

RICHARD FORREST'S LIFE has been characterized by his venturing out, in faith and without funds, whenever he has felt the Lord's definite leading. So it was with his going to Bible school. The three youths shared the offerings of their tent meetings—but that wasn't much. Therefore, it happened that Richard had only carfare to Nyack, New York, where he felt that he had been called to get the Bible training he'd need.

He swung off the train, picked up his telescope, squared his shoulders, and started up the hill to the business office of The Missionary Training Institute, where he hoped to get some help in finding a job.

"Dear Lord, help me find a job. I'm willing to do anything," he prayed as he walked along.

Within a few moments he was ushered into the presence of the business manager of the Institute, a lady, who asked what he wanted.

"A job—anything so that I can stay here and get some training."

"How much money do you have?"

"None—but I'm not afraid of work."

"Why did you come?" she demanded. "You know it costs money to operate a school, and the students have certain fees and other obligations that must be met. How do you figure on paying?"

"I believe the Lord will supply my need and, as I said, I'm willing to work."

"Young man," she replied, "I appreciate your desire for an education and your zeal. But the fact of the matter is that nearly all of the young people who want to come here as students are in circumstances similar to yours. They have no money. How can the Institute pay its bills?"

"Isn't there anyone here in Nyack who needs help? I'll build fires, carry ashes, do anything!"

"I'm telling you, there is no work to be had. I'm sorry, but that's the truth." With that, she turned back to her work.

Richard turned dejectedly and walked slowly from the room. Now what would he do? He was sure God meant for him to be here. Could he be wrong?

Aimlessly he wandered into what was known as the South Parlor, a reception room in the same building. He walked over to a table in the center of the room and glanced down. Without realizing what he was doing, he began reading a newspaper lying on the table, left open at the want ad section. Suddenly he picked up the paper. One "Help Wanted" ad had caught his attention. He reread it: "Wanted—girl to do general housework."

Girl? He could do anything around a house that a girl could. He scanned the page, then looked back to the first ad. It was the only one for which he could at all qualify. Taking his knife out of his pocket, he cut out the notice, pocketed it, and walked quickly from the room.

A few minutes later he was knocking at the door of the home of Miss Sarah A. Staley, a godly Episcopalian woman who was at that time principal of the Greenpoint Public School of Greater New York.

Miss Staley opened the door and looked at the gangling youth standing there. Now, what could this lad want? He looked most uncomfortable, but determined. Then she saw the advertisement in his hand. "Yes?" she encouraged, trying not to smile.

Richard could see the corners of her mouth twitching. He wanted to turn on his heels and run, but he had a determination born of desperation. Holding out the slip of paper, he said, "I came to answer this."

"Are you sure you read it correctly?"

"I thought so." (If only it hadn't so specifically said "girl"!)

"The advertisement calls for a house *girl*, you know."

"Yes, ma'am, but I can do anything about a house that a girl can."

She started to say no—then hesitated. She inspected the boy, from the crown of his head to the soles of his shoes. She noticed his earnestness—the pleading in his eyes.

Then she smiled; and he knew he had the job. He breathed a prayer of thanksgiving.

For two years Richard Forrest worked for Miss Staley. He helped cook, made beds, cleaned, and did many other jobs that a girl couldn't have done, such as mowing the lawn and riddling ashes. (Hard coal was burned, and all that dropped through to the ashes without burning was retrieved.) Another of his duties was taking Miss Staley to the train and bringing her back each day, since she commuted to New York City for her work.

Miss Staley had one idiosyncrasy which affected Richard personally. She could not stand to have a chipped dish in the house. Whenever a chip appeared in a plate, cup, or other dish, Miss Staley would seize the offending article and march out into the back yard. Then, with all her force, she'd hurl the dish smashing against a stone wall.

Richard soon learned that he was expected to pay for any dish that met this untimely doom, and he tried to be as careful as possible, for each penny was precious. His fingers were sometimes clumsy, though, and another cup or plate would sail through the air.

Human nature can stand only so much punishment of a kind, however, before it strikes back. This time it was a plate, the chip hardly noticeable. But Miss Staley's sharp eyes caught the defect. As she snatched the plate and started for the door, Richard called: "Wait, Miss Staley, I'm going to have to pay for that plate. Give me the satisfaction of smashing it."

Miss Staley never smashed another dish so long as Richard worked for her.

It is interesting to note that, when Toccoa Falls Institute was started fourteen years later, Miss Staley retired on a pension and moved to Toccoa Falls, where she offered her services as a teacher as long as she lived. She also built Staley Cottage on a knoll above the lake. It was designated in her will that this cottage be occupied by the Forrests after her death—and there they now reside.

Another friendship made at this home paid dividends later. Miss Staley also had a second youth, Will R. Mc-Duffie, working for her. After some time as a foreign missionary, he came to Golden Valley, North Carolina, as superintendent of the original school there, and later spent several years as superintendent of the Toccoa Falls Institute.

While attending school at Nyack, Richard received an invitation to Cresskill, New Jersey, to preach each Sunday night in the Gospel Hall there. After supper he'd board the train for the twenty-eight mile ride, pondering his subject all the while. His pay each Sunday was a silver dollar. Since train fare amounted to sixty-four cents, after paying that he had thirty-six cents clear; and he often since has remarked with a chuckle that he wasn't worth that. It was here, though, that he made many friends of long standing, friends who have stood behind him and his endeavors down through the years.

One of Richard's hardest testings came just before he graduated from the Institute. One afternoon, while standing on a street corner in New York City, he saw a man who was later president of The Christian and Missionary Alliance. Richard felt definitely called by the Lord to preach and had been looking for a place to serve after his graduation. "Surely," he reasoned, "if anyone can help me, this well-known preacher can." So thinking, he walked over and asked if he could direct him to a church which he might pastor.

To his amazement and chagrin, he heard a reply he hadn't thought possible.

"Richard," kindly answered the gentleman, "you can't preach. I wouldn't discourage you for the world, but in all honesty and fairness I have to tell you, you don't have it in you. God didn't call everyone to preach, my boy, and it seems to me that you'd be far wiser to get a job, become a good Christian layman, and help support those who can preach. That's an honorable profession, too, my lad, and we don't have enough Christian laymen who are concerned with supporting those who can engage in preaching and doing missionary work."

He spoke on, counseling the young man as seemed to him best. Little did he realize that each word was falling like a stone into young Forrest's heart.

As soon as he could courteously do so, Richard parted from his elder. Almost blindly he hurried to his room, where he fell on his face on the carpet and nearly died. All his hopes and aspirations were shattered. What could he do now? Where could he turn? Was he mistaken—had God not called him?

Then he prayed; and God came down from His throne

on high and met His suffering child: "The race is not to the swift, nor the battle to the strong."

"Lord, Thou didst call me? I have heard Thee aright?"

"Yes, my child, go on. Thy promise: 'I can do all things through Christ which strengtheneth me.' "

This was one more lesson taught by the Lord, one of the lessons which would hold him faithful during the following years: listen to God, not to man. Go ahead in spite of obstacles, if the Lord is leading. Furthermore, treat sympathetically anyone in similar circumstances. Never has he told a boy that he was not called to preach. (He feels that the calling is a matter between that lad and God.) On the other hand, if the lad does feel the call, he has done everything in his power to help the boy along the way.

During the first part of Richard's stay at Nyack, Evelyn Drennen was also one of the students. By this time, the two were "going steady". Although sweethearts, they agreed on and engaged in a form of rigid self-discipline and did not take advantage of the privileges granted engaged couples. This, too, has been a lesson which has aided them throughout succeeding years.

It seems that there was a young couple attending Nyack at that time, a couple whose open show of affection was quite sickening to all around. Noticing the reaction of all to these two, Richard wrote to Evelyn, who was two weeks late in entering school, and asked her whether she did not think it would be wise for them not to give any indication that they were interested in each other. She agreed; from September until Christmas time they treated each other almost as strangers. Only once, and then in a group, did they even speak to each other for four months.

At Christmas time they rode home together on the train. There were a number of other Nyack students in the same car—and a great deal of walking past the two with "Why, hello, Richard!" and "How do you do, Miss Drennen!" and

"Fancy seeing you two together!" How sweet it was after that time of self-discipline to acknowledge each other openly!

The lesson? Most of their married life, the Forrests have been separated by the work—he out in evangelistic endeavors, she at home helping take care of the school. Always has the work of the Lord come first; therefore, self-discipline has been a necessity.

In 1900 Miss Drennen completed her work at the Institute. From there she went to Oil City, Pennsylvania, to serve as a full-time Christian worker for The Christian and Missionary Alliance. In her nearly two years there she established a branch of the Alliance in that city and endeared herself to the hearts of the people.

Meanwhile Richard remained in school. During this time there was laid a firm foundation that would prepare him as a missionary on either the foreign or home field. He was used extensively with student groups holding services throughout the metropolitan area and was selected pianist for the chapel services at the school. His ability as a leader was recognized in his being chosen chairman of the Missionary Association, a group that conducted a weekly missionary program and kept the cause of foreign missions before the student body. In these and like endeavors Richard was occupied until the completion of his course in December, 1901.

In the spring of his second year at Nyack, Richard received a letter from Orlando, Florida. "Now whom do I know in Orlando, Florida?" he mused, as he tore open the envelope. A perusal of the contents soon made everything clear and amazed him, as well.

The business manager at Nyack (the very lady who'd turned him away when he had asked for work) was spending her vacation in Orlando. While there she had been asked by friends who were establishing an independent mission in that city to recommend a young man to lead the work there, and she had suggested Richard Forrest! Perhaps this wasn't so astonishing as it seemed, however; for she was a friend of Miss Staley, and had learned somewhat of the determination and drive of this young man who, facing defeat, had the courage and audacity to lay down his pride and apply for—and get—a position as house *girl!* Such a person might be the one to pull together this unorganized group in Orlando and help it bear fruit for the Master.

At any rate the letter, from Mr. John W. Anderson, then elder in the First Presbyterian Church of Orlando, was asking the young Mr. Forrest to become the pastor of the mission.

Elated though he was to think that someone would be issuing him a call, Richard considered and prayed much before answering. Then he wrote, stating that, since he was only twenty, he didn't feel that he was old enough to accept their call.

In October of the same year, the second call came from the same group. Again he answered: "I do not feel that I am old enough to accept your call. I do not have the age or experience."

Then he prayed: "Lord, if the call comes the third time, I'll know that it's Thy will for me to go to Orlando. If they ask me once more, I'll say 'yes.'"

It was early in December when the call came the third time. Richard wrote, accepting, but stating that he had no money. He also mentioned that he was now single, but that he'd rather come to them as a married man. Their immediate answer was that this was ideal: they'd much rather have a married man.

The next item was to write to his fiancée, asking her cooperation in the matter. He told her that he wished to marry her and take her to Orlando with him, but that he

DR. AND MRS. R. A. FORREST—1901 and 1951

had only twenty-seven cents. She replied by the next mail: "I'm not marrying a man for his money." "Well," he thought as he read her response, "that's fortunate." He then began making plans for the wedding, which was to be Christmas Eve.

Although the last days at school seemed to crawl by, there were a number of problems, and they didn't seem to lessen. The principal one was money—or rather, lack of it. The day of his departure dawned, and Richard had only the twenty-seven cents. He needed $3.40 for carfare to Wilmington. "What a dilemma!" he thought. Here he was planning to get married—and he didn't even have enough money to buy a ticket home.

You may call it overboldness, rashness, audacity, or what you will; but to Richard Forrest it seemed simply that God was showing him utter dependence upon Himself. So confident was he that he was being led by God each step of the way that he called a dray and paid the driver a quarter of his precious twenty-seven cents to haul his trunk to the railway station.

During the last few months of his schooling he had moved into the Institute building, and as the time drew near for his train to leave, he began to say farewell to the friends who resided there—still with no money, but still certain that the Lord would provide if he'd step out on faith. What a picture of sweet dependence and utter trust!

It was at this moment that God, through the Reverend A. E. Funk, superintendent of the school, proved Himself. Rev. Funk was a German, a fine Christian man. When Richard came to say good-by, Rev. Funk greeted him thus:

"Vell, vell, my vife und I vanted to gif you somet'ing for your vedding, but you going so far avay—ve t'ought ve'd gif you some money instead."

He handed Richard a five dollar bill. Now he had the answer to this need—money for carfare and a little to spare.

33

So—as he had begun his schooling at Nyack, solely dependent on the Lord and resting absolutely on His faithfulness—in like fashion he was now stepping out from these halls of learning into a life of service for Him.

Chapter Six

"And the Lord God said, It is not good that the man should be alone; I will make him an help meet for him."—GENESIS 2:18

IT WAS ARRANGED that the wedding should be conducted in Miss Drennen's home in Strickersville, Pennsylvania, which was sixteen miles from the Forrest home in Wilmington. Christmas Eve, 1901, was set as the date.

At daybreak Richard Forrest was hitching his uncle's horse to the buggy to start the now familiar trip to his fiancée's home. His uncle had been happy to lend him that horse and buggy many times to go out to see his sweetheart. Today was the climax of all those trips and the beginning of new joys. Enwrapt in visions of their future together, he scarcely noticed the bitter cold, nor did he mind it a bit.

As he traveled, he meditated on some of the seeming obstacles to his marriage and his disposal of each. He reviewed his last conversation with Dr. A. B. Simpson, founder of The Christian and Missionary Alliance. Dr. Simpson admired Miss Drennen, but she had always been frail and delicate. So, when he heard of the forthcoming marriage, Dr. Simpson saw Richard and told him that he questioned the wisdom of their marrying because of her frailty. However, Richard felt that this wedding was in the Lord's will and went on with his plans. And he intended to keep going on, he thought, as he absently watched the ears of the plodding horse.

(It may be of interest here to note that two or three

weeks after their marriage Dr. Simpson wrote to Richard: "I see you've married despite my advice. So now you have my blessing." He enclosed a check, knowing they would need it, and through the years proved a faithful friend.)

There had been a much more serious problem with regard to their marriage, however. Since childhood Evelyn had been wracked with vicious attacks of asthma. As Richard felt that he should go to the mission field if that was the Lord's will, they had a tacit agreement that as long as Evelyn had these asthmatic attacks, they would not marry. Praise God, thought Richard, for an entire year she had not had a single attack. God surely must be pointing toward, and placing His seal upon, their union.

Although Richard did not realize it, God in His providence had been, and would continue to be, through a series of testings, teaching him and his fiancée lessons not learned from books. They were destined to a life of faith involving hundreds of young people passing through the same life cycle, and it would often be necessary for the Forrests to give advice and counsel. As a matter of fact, the next test was to occur within a few moments—even during the morning of their wedding day.

By this time Richard had come within a half mile of the Drennen home. As he came over a rise, he caught the first glimpse of the house. As he drove on, he could see somebody coming out of the front door and he knew it was she— all bundled up. Naturally, he whipped the horse up a bit then.

When he got to the gate, he fastened the horse to the hitch-rail, three or four steps below the level of the lawn. Then he started to dash up the steps, only to stop short in horror as he caught his first glance of her face, shawl-wrapped. His heart sank as he realized that Evelyn was having an attack of asthma!

He didn't know what to do or say, so he said nothing.

Nor did she speak. They just walked into the house together, turned aside into the unheated parlor, and instinctively dropped to their knees at the couch and prayed. Never, in all their lives, do they remember having prayed with more fervor or more desire than they did that day. And God wrought a miracle! For *instantly* the asthma was stopped. Instantly—so quickly that they both were startled. She was breathing normally. She worked hard all day decorating the house with holly and mistletoe and other greens—and the asthma did not come back. They turned to God in their extremity, and He honored them by His healing power.

Evelyn and Richard had planned a very simple service. Had they wished it, an elaborate wedding was out of the question because neither had any money; and yet when the time came, they were amazed at the large number of friends who drove from Wilmington and Newark, and from a number of points in Pennsylvania. During the day Richard's parents had driven out, as well as the Reverend G. Verner Brown, pastor of The Christian and Missionary Alliance Church in Wilmington, who brought a surrey load of people. Among these was Miss Rogers, under whose influence Richard had accepted Christ several years before —and in whose home he had proposed to Evelyn.

The simple, but impressive, ceremony was performed at eight o'clock in the evening, with Rev. Brown in charge. Richard's heart almost burst with joy and pride as he stammered: "I do." Calmly his beautiful bride in turn promised to be his. Throughout more than fifty succeeding years these two have proved to be an ideal couple, "Sweethearts Forever."

The ceremony had scarcely been concluded and God's richest blessing pronounced upon this promising young couple when there was a terrible noise outside. A large number of men and boys—Evelyn's school friends and neighbors—had come to serenade the bride and bridegroom with fish horns, tin pans, and all kinds of noisemaking devices.

Richard's father went to the front door and opened it— he was a large man and nearly filled the doorway. As they peered around him, the newly married couple gazed upon a beautiful sight. Throughout all that day snow had been falling until it was about six inches deep. Every fence post and tree was crowned with white. The men and boys had formed themselves into a semicircle in front of the house, which faced the east. A full moon had risen just high enough to be seen over the treetops, and it glistened on the white mantle of snow, against which the group of black figures stood silhouetted.

For several seconds there was complete silence. Then Richard's father moved to one side, and the bride and bridegroom stepped into the doorway. The silence continued for what seemed a long time. Then a little fellow toward the end of the semicircle took off his hat and cried: "Three cheers for the little preacher and his bride."

As the "little preacher" looked adoringly at his bride, the cheers were given lustily. Then the spell broke, cake was passed around, and everyone had a happy time.

The newly married couple spent their wedding night and the following day—Christmas, 1901—at the home of the bride. Then, early the following morning, Richard hitched his Uncle George's horse to the buggy and they went back to Wilmington together.

There was no such thing as the usual honeymoon since they anticipated a full life span of a honeymoon, but little did they know the supreme test was lurking "just around the corner."

Chapter Seven

"Blessed is the man that endureth temptation: for when he is tried, he shall receive the crown of life, which the Lord hath promised to them that love him."—JAMES 1:12

THE LORD TRIES by fire those who would be His servants; thus He both proves their worth and fits them for service. The Lord was planning to use this young couple mightily; they were destined to face sacrifice, suffering, vicissitudes, disappointments, handicaps, and sorrows. They must be found faithful, ready, and able; they must radiate a sweet Christian testimony despite all trials.

Perhaps it was well that the Forrests did not know, as they walked down Eighth Street in Wilmington, that their first great test as husband and wife was very near. While they strolled along, Evelyn suddenly turned and looked at her husband. Smilingly she said, "You look as if you owned the earth." He agreed with her exactly; he felt that way.

As a matter of fact, in regard to earthly riches, the couple had very little. Richard's father was still bitterly opposed to his going into Christian service; naturally there wasn't much help from him. Evelyn had, perhaps, fared better than her husband. The people with whom she had worked in Oil City were so very, very fond of her that they had "loaded her with benefits"—as far as clothes were concerned. She had everything; therefore Richard didn't have to worry about buying clothes for her for some time.

Just now the great need was money to get to Orlando, in order that they might begin their work. Fortunately, many of their friends said just what Rev. Funk had already told Richard: "You're going so far away and we don't know what to give you, so we decided to give you money." No gift could have been more appreciated.

They were planning to leave for Orlando on January 16, 1902. In the meantime they were to stay with Richard's parents, going to various meetings in the immediate neighborhood. Filled with youthful enthusiasm and boundless hopes, the young couple truly felt that they "owned the earth," as Evelyn had said.

Then came the stunning blow. Just a day or two after their marriage a letter arrived from Mr. J. W. Anderson, chairman of the group who had given the call to Orlando. That letter was full of dynamite, which for a fleeting moment almost shattered the joyous spirit of this newly wed couple. In it Mr. Anderson told of their making different plans whereby they would not need the Forrests in the mission. Rev. R. V. Miller, a nationally known Bible teacher from Hendersonville, North Carolina, had come to Orlando for the winter, and they had asked him to take the work to which they had already called the Forrests. Richard was overwhelmed; here he was with the responsibility of a wife and no place to go!

The young couple didn't know what to do. They had told all their friends their plans for leaving. Farewell parties and meetings were in progress. What should they do? They decided not to mention this matter to anybody except the Lord, but they surely poured out their hearts to Him for help. Furthermore, they'd go to Orlando anyhow and find something to do there. They'd go out independent of any support and trust God to supply their needs. They kept busy going to meetings, proceeding as though everything was going as originally planned.

About a week later they were surprised to receive a second letter from Mr. Anderson. What news could it contain? Feverishly they tore open the envelope and read the contents. Then they had a little prayer meeting of praise and thanksgiving. Mr. Miller had changed his mind and gone back to Hendersonville and "Can you come on right away?" They could!

They hoarded every dime toward their railway tickets. Finally January 15, the day before departure, arrived; and they were still ten dollars short of having enough for carfare. They decided to buy a ticket as far as they could go and then get off the train and get to Orlando as best they could—if they had to walk.

The young people held a combined rally and farewell party that night at Richard's home. The house was filled with folks, and Richard was sure that one of them—or all of them—would make up the necessary ten dollars. However, he trusted the Lord implicitly for his need and said nothing of it to any of the guests. No one offered a cent. No one asked whether a need existed. Finally everyone was gone—and still there was no ten dollars.

It was about ten o'clock when there came a knock at the kitchen door. Richard's heart lifted. Here, he felt sure, came the ten dollars. Then the door opened, and in came his Uncle Sam Forrest. Uncle Sam was a miser and a bachelor. He had never parted willingly with a cent. Richard's heart dropped back into place: there was no answer here. At that moment the uncle called Richard's little brother Edwin, about six, to him, whispered something, handed the child a bit of paper, and pointed to Richard. Then he was gone. Edwin trotted over and handed Richard *a ten dollar bill!*

The Forrests left at four o'clock in the morning. His mother had packed a lunch to last until they got to Orlando the following day. By the time they arrived the cheese was greasy, the eggs runny, and the bread stale; but they were as happy as larks. They never noticed. They went by day coach—that's all they could afford. The car was sooty, and the only place to clean up was at the water cooler at the end of the coach. They would take a handkerchief, get it damp under the faucet, and try to wash off some of the soot and dirt.

When they got off the train, they tried to look as old as possible. After all, he was only twenty. He was wearing a Prince Albert coat with a white string tie. The ends stuck out straight on either side. He was trying to raise a moustache to make him look older—and wasn't succeeding very well. She was dressed in a greyish-brown dress, with a high-boned collar. He had eighty cents in his pocket.

Seventeen people, headed by the Andersons, met them at the station. They sized each other up as they said hello. He could imagine those seventeen people thinking: "Look what we got stuck with!"

The Andersons, with whom Mrs. A. W. Dick, a milliner, lived, took them home to stay with them. When the Forrests were about to enter—even as they started across the threshold into the house—Mr. Forrest put up his hand and said, "Wait a minute. Before we come into your home to live with you, we're going to have an understanding. There are three of you living here. With us, that will be five. I insist on paying two-fifths of the grocery bill."

The Andersons remonstrated with him, telling him that they didn't need or expect help with the bill, that he was a young man just starting out, and so forth; but he still insisted although he had only eighty cents in his pocket and had no knowledge from where any more was coming. Finally everyone agreed to his proposition.

Naturally, Mr. Anderson told the people of the congregation about the matter. As a result, they thought more of the Forrests for their stand. Too, they felt the need of paying their minister although, as a matter of fact, there was no agreement with the mission about money nor was there any salary promised. The work was really one of faith. This independent mission was the first Christian and Missionary Alliance Branch that Mr. Forrest organized as a district superintendent of the Alliance. It later became a Christian and Missionary Alliance Church.

The mode of transportation in 1902 was quite different from that of today. When Rev. Forrest got ten dollars, he bought a second-hand bicycle. Then someone gave him a lady's second-hand bicycle. He and Mrs. Forrest would pack what they'd need in an old blue canvas telescope, he'd strap it on to the handle bars of his bicycle, and off they'd go into the flat woods around Orlando. Sometimes they'd be gone for several weeks at a time. When Mrs. Forrest got too tired pedaling, he'd tie a rope from the back of his bicycle to the handle bars of hers and pull her along until she'd get rested a bit.

They'd go as far as they could each day and stop to talk to people about the Lord. At night they'd stay wherever they happened to be, just like tramps. They'd accept whatever hospitality was offered—and sometimes there was practically nothing to offer. They'd gather together a group of people wherever there were any to listen, hold a meeting, and present the Gospel. In place after place they held meetings like that.

During the two years the Forrests were in Orlando, there were fourteen Sunday schools begun; out of them several churches later were organized. The Forrests worked with the American Sunday School Union representative. The Forrests would win the people to the Lord; then the Sunday School Union man would organize them into Sunday-school groups. Although they were young and inexperienced and ignorant about what to teach, the Sunday School Union supplied literature to them and they persevered. It was a fine job—a wonderful piece of work they were doing. However, this was real pioneer work; and as such it called for real sacrifice, labor, and love for the Lord.

It was during these two years that Richard Forrest reached his point of greatest testing. For him it was the crisis—this was the time when he felt at the lowest ebb and was, for the only time in his life, ready to give up that to which he had dedicated himself: full-time Christian service.

He didn't want to accept a salary. He had the mistaken idea that that would mean he'd be working for the people instead of God. As a result, the Forrests had some lean times. This time they had come back to Orlando from a six-weeks' trip out in the flat-woods country. There was no food in their rooms, for they didn't want mice and ants coming in while they were gone. There was no icebox, of course.

They arrived at home at nine-thirty at night, having pedaled in on their bicycles. As they were getting ready to retire, Mrs. Forrest asked her husband how much money he had. He answered, "None; I spent the last for our supper." She reminded him that there was nothing in the house for breakfast. Of course, they had many friends who would have supplied them, but they didn't want to beg.

They got down on their knees. The devil kept talking to Rev. Forrest and taunting him. He prayed, but all he could think of to tell the Lord was what a failure he was. Finally, as the devil kept goading him, he told the Lord that he wouldn't be a preacher, that after breakfast the next morning he'd go hunt a job. He was worse than an infidel— he couldn't even take care of the lovely wife he'd been given. First Timothy 5:8 rang through his mind: *But if any provide not for his own, and specially for those of his own house, he hath denied the faith, and is worse than an infidel.*

44

All the time her husband was praying thus, Mrs. Forrest was thanking the Lord for all His benefits and begging Him: "Don't let Richard be discouraged."

Finally they went to bed. Each was trying to lie very quietly, endeavoring to convince the other that he was asleep. Each knew the other wasn't asleep.

At last Rev. Forrest must have slept, for the next thing he realized was that Mrs. Forrest was shaking him and telling him to get up. Someone was knocking on the back door.

He opened the door and was startled to see, standing on the steps and holding a basket in one hand and a jug in the other, Mr. George E. Macy, a Georgia countryman who had moved to Florida and made money. Mr. Macy, a rough, kind-hearted man, owned a carriage factory, a grist mill, a syrup mill, and a rice-shelling mill.

The Macys kept roomers. A little after 9:30 the night before, a roomer came through the parlor on his way to his quarters and casually said, "I just saw the Forrests ride into town."

As Mr. Macy was getting ready for bed, he thought: "I wonder if those children have anything in the house to eat." He went to bed, but couldn't sleep. He tossed and turned; at 2 a.m. he got up and packed a basket. Then he sat and waited for daylight, so he could take the basket and jug to the Forrests. With tears in his eyes he said, "Let me tell you, if you make me lose a good night's sleep again worrying about you, you'll hear about it from me."

The Forrests have never forgotten the contents of that basket. There were one-half dozen eggs, one-half dozen oranges, some grapefruit, a pineapple, a bag of grits, and a bag of rice. The jug contained one-half gallon of syrup—for just two people.

As soon as Mr. Macy left, the Forrests again knelt in prayer. This time, however, Mrs. Forrest was praising God for answering her prayers of the night before and supplying their needs; Rev. Forrest was thanking God for His goodness and asking forgiveness for his doubts of the previous evening.

Never since that time has Rev. Forrest ever felt the slightest doubt as to his calling. God, in answering His child and guiding him through this crucial moment, showed him beyond the shadow of a doubt that his feet were on the right path, that his task in life was to serve the Almighty. The way has sometimes been dim, the nights have been black, problems have surrounded and almost overwhelmed him at times—but Richard Forrest has pressed steadily forward, knowing that *the steps of a good man are ordered by the Lord: and he delighteth in his way.*

Chapter Eight

"Let no man despise thy youth; but be thou an example of the believers, in word, in conversation, in charity, in spirit, in faith, in purity."—I Timothy 4:12

From 1902 to 1911 God put the Forrests through a school of preparation for the greater task—the labor which was to occupy most of their years of service for Him. This training period was, in itself, abundantly fruitful. Many souls were won into His kingdom; religious groups were established; churches were revived and revitalized; miracles became almost the expected rather than the unusual occurrence. The Master's hand was evident in every event—leading His dear ones on—training and teaching them—until they would be able to catch the vision He had for them and, having understood His plan, carry it out despite all obstacles, looking unto Him for the solution to each problem or trial.

It was during these early years that Richard Forrest began his work as an evangelist—the work by means of which he has been endeared to many, won hundreds and hundreds of souls to the Lord and to fruitful Christian service, and made the work of Toccoa Falls Institute known to thousands.

His music helped to "put him over" in a great many places. He played the organ and piano very well, and also sang a good deal. Those who have heard him play and sing such numbers as "Li'l Brack Sheep" will never forget them. He also liked to lead song services and, in a sense, "put on his own show." It helped in many, many places where the people wouldn't come just to hear a preacher. They'd come for the other things and then get the preaching besides.

Like many another young preacher, Rev. Forrest often had more zeal than knowledge, more boldness than discretion. At one time he received a letter from a Northern Presbyterian Church at Winter Haven, Florida. In effect, the letter stated that the American Sunday School Union representative had recommended him as evangelist for a series of meetings, and would he come? Although Winter Haven was then a very small place, young Forrest went there in fear and trembling. He didn't know what he was going to do. He had about a dozen sermons that he preached over and over again. Had he realized what was in store during the next few days, he'd probably have taken the next train back to Orlando.

He stayed at the home of the pastor, whose wife was a very vain, very attractive woman about twenty-five years younger than her husband. He was an old gentleman with white whiskers, except for a brown streak right down the middle—the result of chewing tobacco and drooling. Rev. Forrest arrived on Saturday and heard him preach on Sunday morning. The old man had a box with sand in it on the platform. From the pulpit he could hit that sand box every time—between every sentence, it seemed to the boyish preacher. How revolting! How could he do it? thought the young man, who was dead set against tobacco.

Rev. Forrest began meetings that night. The church, a nice little brick building, was crowded. There were twenty-odd young men there who were known as pickers. They'd drift from place to place and pick whatever crop had matured at that time—first a bean crop, then an orange crop, then a celery crop, and so on. These pickers were in the meeting for a good time. They had broken up two series of meetings before this one in this same church.

Although a youth himself, Rev. Forrest immediately detected the undercurrent of the meeting. He also felt the cold formality of the pastor and the regular church goers. As a youngster, he had the idea that something drastic would have to be done to break up the spirit of the pickers and to break down the coldness of the regular congregation. Therefore, when it was time to pray, he insisted that everybody kneel. Such a procedure had never been suggested in that church before—never! At first no one moved. Then Rev. Forrest stated decisively: "We shall not pray until everybody is on his knees."

Everyone knelt! The entire crowd of pickers were the first to fall on their knees—a little tittering among them, of course. The last person to kneel was the preacher's wife, and Rev. Forrest could imagine he could hear her bones creak as she was getting down on her knees. Angry—she was furious! Although his hostess, she never spoke to him again until Friday night. If she had anything to say to him, even while they were sitting at the same table, she'd tell her husband, "You tell this man Forrest so-and-so"; then he'd repeat what she had just said.

The meeting, as can be imagined, was dead. People continued to come in order to see what Rev. Forrest would do next. Finally, on Thursday night, he became desperate. Friday morning he borrowed the pastor's old sorrel horse and rickety old buggy. All day long he went around the community, stopping at private homes. He didn't know who was going to that church and who wasn't, so he talked to all he saw. He found everybody in the community at odds with everybody else. All was in turmoil, and all were angry at the preacher's wife. She'd antagonized the folks everywhere around. That night he went to church "loaded."

The meeting began as usual, with the opening songs and prayers and scripture reading. Then, blundering ahead in the manner of youth, Rev. Forrest said, "Now, I'm not go-

49

ing to preach a word until we have some confessions around here." Then he told the congregation what he had found on that trip around the neighborhood that day and what people had to say about each other. He even called names. It was the most unheard of thing; people gasped, then wriggled uncomfortably, then became absolutely silent. The youthful evangelist concluded his remarks somewhat as he had begun: "We're not going to have any more singing or preaching or praying until confessions are made." With that he bowed his head over the Bible and closed his eyes.

For the longest time not a person moved. Not a sound was heard. Meanwhile he was praying that the people would be touched. Also he was wondering what to do if no one moved. He decided that he could stand there as long as they could sit. At length, he heard someone over to his left stir. He peeped. It was the pastor's wife. She got up and went across the church to a lady who was sitting to the far right. She put her arm across the lady's shoulders and whispered something into her ear. Rev. Forrest never found out what she said, but the next minute the two women were clasped in each other's arms, and bedlam broke loose in the church. They had a wonderful time! Twenty-one of those pickers came forward that night and knelt at the front row of seats and there accepted the Lord. Besides these boys there were one old man and one woman converted.

Rev. Forrest had been ready to conclude the series of meetings that night, but after the events just mentioned, the meetings went on for days and days. Everyone had a blessed time. The pastor's wife couldn't do enough for the youthful evangelist; she was wonderful to him.

Thus was God pleased to honor the labors of His servant. In like manner, He has placed His seal of approval on Dr. Forrest's evangelistic efforts throughout many parts of the world.

In Bible school work, a host of friends and prayer part-ners throughout the country is an invaluable asset. With his catching chuckle, his overflowing enthusiasm, and his rare personality, Dr. Forrest has made scores and scores of friends through the years.

During his years at The Missionary Training Institute, Richard Forrest had come under the notice of Dr. A. B. Simpson, founder of The Christian and Missionary Alliance and pastor of their church in New York City. After the Forrests moved to Florida, Dr. Simpson sent them yearly steamship tickets north for the annual convention at Old Orchard, Maine. As Dr. Simpson's protege, Rev. Forrest often supplied his pulpit—one year for two months straight. He made many friends of many years' standing at the con-ventions and in Dr. Simpson's church.

Dr. Simpson also called upon the young man to preach in other churches of the Alliance besides his own. It was while on the way back to Orlando from one of these engage-ments that he was able to make contacts and introduce the Alliance in Savannah, Georgia.

Rev. Forrest had been preaching up North. The engage-ment wasn't so remunerative as he had expected; as a con-sequence he didn't have enough money to get back home. In those days there was a great deal of travel north and south by boat; as this mode of travel was less expensive than the train, he decided to take a ship to Savannah from Philadelphia. He wrote a letter to Mrs. Forrest, who was in Orlando, telling her what day he'd arrive in Savannah and asking her to send him some money there so that he could get the rest of the way home. Then he boarded the ship, The Old Savannah Line.

After three or four days of leisurely travel, he arrived in Savannah without any money. He immediately went to the Post Office and inquired for mail at the General Deliv-ery window. To his dismay, there was no letter. He didn't know what to do. He had no money to stay at a hotel; as a matter of fact, he couldn't even buy himself anything to eat.

He was not one to sit around feeling sorry for himself, though. If he couldn't eat, at least he could work. As sole representative of the Alliance in the south during those days, he was eager to establish as many churches in as many places as possible. Everywhere he went he carried a list of subscribers to the "Christian Alliance," now "The Alliance Weekly." He got out his list and scanned it. There was just one subscriber in Savannah, a Dr. Clay. Rev. Forrest called on him and was invited to stay for dinner. Naturally, he accepted the invitation.

After dinner and a fine talk, he went back to the Post Office. Altogether he visited the General Delivery window four times that day. At last, at a quarter to six in the evening, there was a letter for him. It was not from Mrs. Forrest, however, but from a lady in Ossining, New York. As a member of the Alliance Board of Managers, she had just been to a board meeting in New York. There Dr. Simpson had told about Richard Forrest's being North for a preaching engagement and returning as far as Savannah by boat. "I don't know whether he has enough money to get from there to Orlando," Dr. Simpson casually mentioned.

On the way from New York to Ossining, the lady felt that the Lord was definitely telling her to write a note to Rev. Forrest and send it to Savannah. At first she decided to wait until she got home; then she thought: "No, it's the time to do it right now." She wrote the letter on the train, enclosed ten dollars, and mailed it in a railway station. She sent the letter to R. A. Forrest, General Delivery, Savannah. It was the wildest kind of guess that he would get it. Furthermore, in her hurry she put no return address on the envelope.

The ten dollars was enough to get him to Orlando; however, he stayed all night with Dr. and Mrs. Clay before starting out. Such was the introduction of the Alliance to Savannah. Rev. Forrest went back there after that because the Clays knew him.

You may feel that this incident is most unusual in that similar occurrences were undoubtedly very rare. You would be in error, for of these times Dr. Forrest later testified: "Oh, I had things like that almost daily; we had the most amazing times."

During their two years in Florida, Richard Forrest was made the first District Superintendent of the Alliance in the South. His salary was $25.00 a month. There was no transportation nor office provided. His territory included the region from Washington, D. C., to El Paso, Texas. This region has since been divided into three districts.

In 1904 a missionary conference was held at Atlanta. Dr. Simpson was the director, and he insisted that the Forrests come up to the meeting. There they met Dave Fant, Ulysses Lewis, and many other Atlantians who later became close friends. It was at this conference that the Forrests were persuaded to move to Atlanta and make their headquarters there.

For several months they lived on Luckie Street in Dave Fant's home. During this time Rev. Forrest used to rock David Fant, Junior, to sleep. He also taught him his first lessons on the organ while he was still a little boy. David is now the General Secretary of the New York Bible Society. The Fants were very kind to the Forrests and have always been wonderful friends.

The Forrests later moved to South Pryor temporarily and then to Capitol Avenue, where they had only one room in which to live and only an open fireplace for heating and over which to cook. Richard rigged up a grate on which to cook eggs. It was hard living for a while.

Rev. Forrest has always had the faculty of making friends easily. Although he was reared in the North, the folks of the South and of Atlanta, in particular, immediately opened their hearts to him. For this reason and because of his opening up places and having conventions, the work in Atlanta was much enlarged.

The Forrests actually built The Christian and Missionary Alliance organization of Atlanta. They started in a second-floor lodge room on North Broad Street. It was not long until the little prayer band outgrew these quarters. Feeling the need of expansion and a place of their own, they purchased a five-room home at 79 Capitol Avenue, one-half block from the state capitol building. They pitched a large canvas tent in the back yard of the lot during the summer to use as a meeting place until they tore out the partitions of the house and remodeled it to use as a church building. Theirs was a humble group, none of whom had much money.

The group owed $4,500.00 on this new property and were praying for it, for the note would fall due in a few days. During this time, Rev. Forrest visited and preached in Hatboro, Pennsylvania, on the outskirts of Philadelphia. At the conclusion of the service an old blind man came up to him and asked where he could put some money. Well, Rev. Forrest knew where he could put some, and told the old man about the need in Atlanta. When he went home, he carried the blind man's check for $4,500.00 in his pocket.

He did not tell anyone that he had the money. The next Sunday afternoon a large crowd gathered in the tent to pray for the money needed to pay the note. They talked about the need, then bowed their heads and began to pray as Rev. Forrest got up to speak. He reminded them of the amount of their obligation and so forth; then, very quietly, he said: "I have a check to the amount of $4,500.00 in my coat pocket."

Heads jerked up—then as they got the import of his statement, joy prevailed. Charlie Burge, the treasurer, was the first to grasp the significance of the statement, and he was so happy that he started to shinny up the tent pole, shouting, "Glory, glory, glory!"

Bedlam broke loose. Mr. Lewis, an attorney, in his nasal drawl, cried, "Praise the Lord!" They had a wonderful time that day—and paid the note on time.

Later, on the same spot they built a tabernacle that seated eight hundred people. Rev. Forrest pastored that church for several years. It was there that Mrs. Forrest, commuting from Toccoa Falls, had one of her many large Bible classes.

Although more than busy in Atlanta and the regions round about, Rev. Forrest could not forget that the district of which he was superintendent extended as far west as Texas, and he wanted to get to Texas. He had a habit of making contacts in new regions through subscribers to the "Christian Alliance" (as has been mentioned), and there were twelve subscribers in all of Texas. He and Mrs. Forrest were praying that he could "break into Texas."

There was an Alliance Home in Atlanta by this time. Friends going through the city could stay at this home much more cheaply than in a hotel—and have fellowship, too.

On one occasion a Texas judge and his wife stopped there. He was dying of tuberculosis and was on his way from Washington to his home in Houston. His wife came to Rev. Forrest and said: "I know it's foolish of me to ask you, but would you consent to go to Houston on the train with us? I need someone to take care of the judge. But I'll tell you now, I can afford to buy only a one-way ticket for you."

He went home and asked Mrs. Forrest what to do. She answered, "You've been praying to go to Texas; you never said anything about coming back." He went.

When they arrived at Houston, the judge's brother met

55

them at the station. With his obligation discharged, Rev.
Forrest found a room for the night. As to money, he had
ten dollars in a long wallet which he carried in an inside
coat pocket. Also in the wallet was the list of the twelve
names of the Alliance subscribers in Texas. Besides the
ten dollars, he had three or four dollars in his trousers
pocket.

That evening he wrote postcards to eleven of the subscribers. The twelfth was a shoemaker who lived in Galveston. He decided to go see him personally.

He bought a round trip ticket to Galveston. When he
got there, he found a circus in town. As he was making
his way through the huge crowd, a pickpocket stole his
long wallet, containing his ten dollars and his return ticket,
as well as the names of the subscribers. How fortunate it
was that he'd already written and mailed those postcards!

He had enough money to get back to Houston. There
he found a card from the wife of General William Stacey
of Austin, asking him to come to Austin. He had no money
to buy a ticket, so he went to the Associated Charities,
where he met a lovely lady, a Mrs. Gray. He asked for a
loan of five dollars on one condition: that he would send
it back as soon as possible. Mrs. Gray responded that she'd
lend him some money on two conditions: first, that it would
be ten dollars, and second, that he not return it. He answered that he'd take the ten dollars but insisted on sending that sum back. They had a lovely visit and prayer.

Rev. Forrest arrived at Austin on Wednesday noon and
looked up the Staceys. General Stacey was a steward in
the Methodist Church; Mrs. Stacey was a very godly woman. They took him to prayer meeting at the Methodist
Church that evening. Rev. Forrest was asked to speak,
and that was one time that "the fire fell." They had a
marvelous time, a real Pentecost. The pastor decided to
have meetings each night, and on Sunday night the church
was packed.

On the way home after the service, General Stacey asked: "Brother Forrest, who pays your expenses? You haven't taken an offering or said one thing about money. Why, I have a pocket full of money for you. Do you remember having a sweet, plain old lady pull your head down and whisper something into your ear?"

"Yes," he replied.

"She is Mrs. R. T. Hill. She's also very rich. She handed me one hundred dollars and asked me to see that you got it."

Rev. Forrest sent the ten dollars back to the Associated Charities of Houston.

On this trip he preached for such notables as Dr. Frank Norris of the First Baptist Church of Fort Worth; Dr. C. I. Scofield, pastor of the Congregational Church in Dallas and later editor of the Scofield Bible; and Fred Bosworth, the famous evangelist, who was then a local preacher in Texas. He also met John A. Hubbard, who later assisted him for a number of years at Toccoa Falls Institute.

Day by day in sundry ways, of which the instances above are typical, God was educating, encouraging, and enabling His servants to carry out the task which He had for them, held in abeyance until He should judge them ready. Very soon now He would indicate to them the larger assignment.

Chapter Nine

"Go forward."—EXODUS 14:15

"Feed my lambs."—JOHN 21:15

"—teaching every man in all wisdom; that we may present every man perfect in Christ Jesus."—COLOSSIANS 1:28

SOMETIMES THE LORD, in a spectacular way, makes known His will to His children; sometimes, on the other hand, through many seemingly minor events, He brings a growing conviction that something should be done about a critical situation.

It was by means of the second method that God began to speak to Rev. and Mrs. Forrest (separately) concerning the establishment of a school for the purpose of giving educational advantages to those who never had them, plus Bible teaching and training for Christian workers.

This "growing conviction" is best summarized in the Toccoa Falls Institute's first catalog, printed in 1911:

> "Some years ago in a providential way, doors began to open for aggressive mission work among coal mining camps, cotton mill towns, and mountain districts of the South. As the work progressed and souls were saved, there arose a crying need among the young men and women who became Christians. They were anxious to help others, yet found themselves unable to do so to any considerable extent, because they never had educational opportunities. Some of them were not able to read or write, yet among them are some of the noblest and brightest characters one could meet. As

they have come to us to ask for a chance to learn something of the Bible and of the English language, that they may help others, they have powerfully appealed to us. The demand for a school into which we could take these young men and women and give them an opportunity to get a Christian education, became so great that it gave much concern."

It was while Rev. Forrest was turning over in his mind how such a school could be established, and by whom, that he went to Jacksonville, Alabama, to preach. Among those saved in the meetings was a young man, J. F. Dunn. After his conversion, he went to Rev. Forrest and told him that the Lord had called him to preach, but that he had no way of studying and equipping himself. Since he had gone to work in a cotton mill before reaching the age of ten, he had only a third grade education.

It was this boy's intense desire for knowledge that crystallized Rev. Forrest's interest in getting someone to found a school where a boy like that who wanted to preach could get his training. Still he had no thought of starting or running such a school himself.

Upon his return to Atlanta, he attended a Wednesday night prayer meeting in the North Avenue Presbyterian Church. There he mentioned the young man whom he'd met in Alabama and told of his plight.

The next day Miss Elizabeth Trailer, a very prominent socialite, called upon Rev. Forrest. She stated that she hadn't been able to sleep the night before because of thinking about that boy. "There should be a place—a school—started where a boy like that could go," she said and, pointing her finger emphatically at Rev. Forrest, added: "and you ought to start it!"

Although he had been aware of the need, up to that time Rev. Forrest had never dreamed of beginning such a work. Before he could remonstrate, however, Miss Trailer continued, "I have no money, but I brought something here that you can turn into money if you'll accept it to start such a school." She handed him two beautiful diamond earrings.

Rev. Forrest thought of this challenge for some time before mentioning it to his wife. He wasn't sure that she'd feel led in the same direction. Imagine his surprise, then, when she confessed to him that she had been doing much thinking about the same thing. Meanwhile, the diamonds had been sold in New York for $300.00. This formed the beginning of a fund which was later used toward the purchase of school property.

During their search for a place to start a school for under-privileged boys and girls—and adults who needed and desired an education—the Forrests heard of a place called Golden Valley, North Carolina, where there was the frame-work of a building. They decided to use their nest egg to buy it, finish it, and establish their school there.

Mr. Will R. McDuffie, a Scotchman from Braden County, North Carolina, was obtained to run the school. He and Richard Forrest had been roommates at Nyack and were good friends. He used to pray: "Oh, Lord, make us a correct translation of Thy Word." Once Richard asked him what he meant by that. He answered, "Well now, we read that we're living epistles known and read of all men; it would be too bad if we were incorrect translations." Such a man first headed the school.

Mr. McDuffie had married Lillian Stemm, Evelyn's room-mate at school. In answer to the mission call, they went to the Sudan to Sierre Leone and served there for one full term of four years. Then they had to return home because of the health of both of them.

On hearing that they would be unable to return to the field, Rev. Forrest got in touch with them, asking them to come to Golden Valley to take charge of the school. They lived there and did most of the building. The Forrests remained in Atlanta, living in the one room where they did their cooking over the open grate. They, in a sense, "commuted" to Golden Valley and helped finish the building. The women, too, nailed on the laths and boards. Everybody worked and was happy to do it.

It was seventeen miles to a railroad; travel to town and back took from dawn to night. All the furniture for the school and living quarters had to be carried in by wagon. The road was so steep that in some places it was all the horses could do to pull the empty wagon to the top of the hill. The men would have to unload the wagon, carry each piece of furniture uphill, and then reload.

There were about thirty students at Golden Valley. One of the first was J. F. Dunn, the boy from Alabama whose need spurred on the venture. Later, when the school was moved to Toccoa, he continued his studies there. He afterward became a very prominent preacher in the Methodist Church. Rev. Forrest preached for him when he was pastor of the Walker Memorial Methodist Church in Birmingham, a very large, lovely church, and was entertained at the Dunn home for dinner. As Rev. Forrest was leaving, Rev. Dunn took his hand in one of his and his wife's in the other and said, "Honey, the Lord surely has been good to us, hasn't He? If it hadn't been that your husband met this man, he would still be an illiterate working in a cotton mill." Rev. Dunn was a presiding elder in Alabama two or three times, yet when he came to Golden Valley he could scarcely read or write. He was one of the trophies of the **work.**

Before long it became evident that the school needed to be on a railroad, more accessible to everyone. For some time the Forrests made inquiry as to a better site.

One of the members of their church in Atlanta was Dave Fant, railway engineer. Having lived in Toccoa a number of years, he knew of the popular resort hotel, Haddock Inn, situated about two miles north of the town. Recently Mr. Fant had heard that the Inn was for sale and casually told his wife. She in turn passed the news along to the Forrests and suggested that they investigate. The result of this investigation has been narrated in Chapter One.

Richard Forrest never could remember what was said on the way back to Toccoa after that memorable transaction. His heart leaping with joy, he boarded the train for Atlanta. True, he'd obligated himself to a debt of $24,990.00; but the Lord would help him pay that. At last, they had an ideal setup for their Bible school.

However, the events of the following days almost punctured the balloon of hope, for problems soon began to assert themselves. The first was the actual transfer of property. Rev. Forrest went at once to see Mr. Ulysses Lewis, a lawyer friend and member of his Atlanta church. The result was recorded by Mrs. Forrest in her diary:

> "Everybody crosswise. Looks like the Toccoa property is gone, on account of the title."

Nevertheless, the men continued to work, and about nine days later Mrs. Forrest wrote:

> "Richard spent the whole day in Mr. Lewis' office helping to make out the papers for the Toccoa property."

Shortly after acquiring Haddock Inn, the Forrests felt the necessity of being there themselves. In the afternoon of February 1, 1911, they were driven out to Haddock Inn by some friends in Toccoa. Mrs. Forrest's entry in her diary that evening read:

> "Supper was our first meal here and we rejoiced over really being here at last."

They lived from meal to meal at first, not even from day to day but from meal to meal. There was nobody else living near except the man who ran the power plant and who lived with his family in a shack nearby.

First purchases for Toccoa Falls Institute were meager. A memorandum records the following expenses:

2/1/1911—Stove, axe, and cooking utensils	. .	$14.50
2/10 —Tub, knives, and washboard	. . . .	1.50
2/10 —Wood	. . . .	1.50

In reminiscing, Dr. Forrest says of these early days: "We didn't even have a chicken. How we lived, I cannot remember. We were getting an allowance of $25.00 a month on which to live—as district superintendent. That was paid pro rata, which means that if it wasn't there when time to pay, it wasn't paid. But we had no complaint; rather we were hilariously happy. What dreams I dreamed; what visions I had for the school!"

Rev. Forrest proved to be more than a visionary; while his head was in the clouds, his feet were on the ground. He realized that, before the students could be moved from Golden Valley to Toccoa Falls, Haddock Inn must have a central heating plant. He made known this fact to Mr. Lewis, the attorney who had helped make out the papers for the transfer.

Just at this time, the Fulton County Courthouse in Atlanta was being torn down, in order to build a new one. Through the help of Mr. Lewis, the heating plant was retrieved from that building for Haddock Inn. Mr. Rinehardt, a Roman Catholic from Atlanta, kindly installed the boiler and registers before the students arrived. (This gentleman spent and still spends an hour a day before the altar of his church in prayer—and Dr. Forrest's name is on his prayer list. He remembers him and the school every day.)

When the students were moved in, the building was well-heated and comfortable all the time, although the halls were large and wide. At first wood was used; afterward they "got highbrow" and used coal part of the time. The coal was brought in a wagon load at a time.

Getting the money to pay for the steam heating plant was a main concern. It came from Mrs. C. M. Rowland of Orlando, one of the mission group there. Her husband had been a doctor; at his death he left her more than $70,000.00. She lost every bit of it except her house and $10,000.00. While vacationing at Haddock Inn during the summer of 1911, she came to Rev. Forrest one day with an unusual proposition: would he take her $10,000.00 and pay her interest on it for the rest of her life? He was afraid to take the money—she'd lost all the rest, and he was afraid to take the remainder for fear he'd lose that. Finally he compromised and told her he'd take half of it as an annuity and pay her six per cent interest, which was $25.00 a month. This money made it possible to install the heating plant, which cost $6,000.00.

About the middle of March, 1911, the buildings and property at Golden Valley were sold to the Southern Baptist Church, and were used as a school there until some time later, when need for railroad facilities caused the move to Nebo.

In March Mr. and Mrs. McDuffie, the other teachers, and the students moved from Golden Valley to Toccoa Falls and were installed in Haddock Inn. There was a large chapel and lecture room on the third floor; and men and women lived on separate floors, each using a different staircase. In this way "our large family can enjoy the home atmosphere without being crowded or unnecessarily thrown together," stated an early catalog.

During the days before the school was moved, the Forrests worked unceasingly in order to have everything in readiness. Mrs. Forrest confided to her diary:

> "Well, we would like to do everything at once; there is so much to be done that one is bewildered, not knowing which way to start first."

In addition to getting the heating plant installed, the Forrests had to take inventory, clean the fifty rooms of Haddock Inn, see that furniture was moved and plans completed on housing the students—allocating classroom and dormitory space, setting up facilities for feeding the students and doing their laundry, and handling countless other incidental problems.

The need for money was always with them. Nobody in Toccoa would trust the school for a dime, at first. This was a venture in faith, and the businessmen naturally would hesitate to extend credit until they could reasonably expect to be paid. The student body was comprised of poor folks, the very purpose of the school being to help those who could not get help through regular channels. Only eight or ten of the students had a little money; the rest were in school on faith. The charge made to those who could pay seems absurd today. On pages eight and nine of the first catalog are these statements concerning expenses:

> "The expenses have been fixed at so low a rate that the poorest applicant who has any ambition at all need not stay away and neglect his education on account of money. Board and tuition are furnished at the Institute for $10.00 a month, payable each month in advance. This amount covers regular table board, furnished room, heat, light, and household laundry; also full tuition except music.
>
> "Music is extra. Private lessons on the organ or piano will be given by a competent teacher for 25 cents per lesson.

"On account of the low rate of board and tuition, each student will be required to work 12 hours each week at some kind of work about the household or premises under the direction of those in charge. Some energetic students will doubtless be able to work more time than this, and for each hour over the prescribed 12 hours per week will receive 8 cents per hour. Students may be relieved of the 12 hours work by paying $1.00 per week extra; but this is not advised, as the household and farm work is intended to contribute in some degree to the completeness of the student's training."

Practically no one ever paid the dollar a week to keep from working; on the other hand, most of the students were happy to whittle down their bills by working overtime, *at 8 cents per hour.* Everybody did work in those days—and rejoiced in the opportunity to do so.

One of the ways by which the Forrests sought to obtain a little money to keep the school going was in renting extra rooms in Haddock Inn to vacationists. Board and room was advertised at one dollar per day, if arranged for in advance. Prayer went up constantly, especially during that first summer, for guests—and praise when the guests came. Unexpected visitors sometimes caught Mrs. Forrest unawares. Since there was never enough money to keep a well-stocked pantry, sometimes the next meal was delayed until someone could go to town for groceries.

"Well, we are in a dilemma sure enough," Mrs. Forrest wrote one Sunday morning in her diary, "the house full of folks and nothing to give them to eat."

She was always able to cope with any situation, nonetheless, and later in the day she noted: "Brother Dunn and I had a fine mountain trip hunting for food. No vegetables in the country. Four more men came just for the day."

The next day she supervised the planting of a garden.

Mr. Forrest also labored prodigiously. He has always believed that honest labor goes hand in hand with prayer in the working out of any enterprise. One of his early tasks was bringing out the groceries and other necessary supplies from town. Until they got a horse, he carried the groceries the two miles from Toccoa on his back. One time he decided to get "right stylish" and buy some rubbers. He put on his new rubbers, hoisted a fifty-pound sack of flour onto one shoulder, picked up a heavy basket of groceries in his other hand, and started home. It was a sea of mud between Toccoa and Toccoa Falls. Just below the place where the dairy barns are now situated there used to be a knoll, called Indian Cemetery. Right there Mr. Forrest's rubbers pulled off in the mud. He couldn't set the flour down in the mud, nor could he put the groceries down, so he had to walk out of the rubbers and on home. Later he went back and retrieved them.

In the spring of 1911 a boy came driving in from Elmore, Alabama. He had a horse named Nellie hitched to a wagon, the wheels of which wobbled in every direction. He wanted to trade Nellie for an education. The transaction was completed, and the Institute now owned a horse and a wagon of a sort. Six months later Nellie gave birth to a beautiful colt, which was named Prince.

At this time, also, the school bought a cow. Mrs. Forrest and Ora Frost, one of the first students, milked the cow—many times in the rain. Finally, a little shed was built for her on what is now called "The Old Ball Field." Sam and Henry, two steers, were obtained meanwhile, and were used for a number of years.

Miss Sarah A. Staley, the school teacher for whom Rev. Forrest had worked while attending Nyack, arrived in Toccoa on the same day as the Forrests did and worked with them—helping, exhorting, counseling, and teaching until the time of her death. Shortly after her arrival, she built Staley Cottage on a knoll overlooking the campus.

During the first two years of the school's existence, progress became evident. Enough money, in small amounts, was contributed to pay five thousand dollars on the $25,000 debt on the building and property. Early in 1913 construction was begun on a barn (now Morrison Hall). An excellent group of teachers had been obtained. More students were entering the Institute for training. Everyone was happy: it seemed that the survival and success of the school were established.

Perhaps the reason for the early flourishing of Toccoa Falls Institute is best summarized by Mr. Dave Fant: "This whole place was born in real consecration and prayer. Forrest is a man who would venture out to do anything that was right. He worked marvelously, made friends, and people gave him money in ways that you couldn't think of to carry on."

Chapter Ten

*"Beloved, think it not strange concerning the fiery trial
which is to try you . . . . . but rejoice."*—1 PETER 4:12, 13

PERHAPS THE LORD felt that things were running too
smoothly for the folks at Toccoa Falls Institute and was
concerned lest they trust in themselves and lose sight of
Him; more than likely Satan was before the throne of God
accusing the brethren, and God allowed him to prove His
children. Whatever the reason, a series of trials and testings of faith were to come in quick succession to Rev.
Forrest and those associated with the Institute.

Without warning, on March 7, 1913, tragedy first struck.
It was ten o'clock in the morning. Everybody was in
class. Miss Staley was on the way down hill from her
house to Haddock Inn for her class. She glanced casually
toward the Inn, then stood transfixed in horror: the roof
of the building was a mass of flames. She was so excited
that she couldn't cry out and so weak that she couldn't
walk; she just had to sit down on the hillside, completely
paralyzed. Finally the thought of everyone inside the Inn
roused her to action, and she hurried on down the hill,
calling all the time for somebody to come.

In the meantime someone else had discovered the fire.
The fire underwriters said later that the cause of the
fire was as follows: when the chimney was built in 1911
it encountered what is called a king beam, made of fat
pine. Whether it was the fault of the contractor or the
brick mason, the fact remained that the beam was built

into the chimney, not into the smoke passage itself, yet with only one course of brick between. There was not enough mortar right at this point. Soot got in where the mortar should have been. After two years the soot finally caught fire and the building burned.

The fat pine beam burned like tinder, and the entire building was of the same material. In just a few minutes the Inn was a conflagration. Everything the students and teachers had went up in smoke. There had been six pianos—everything was now one pile of rubbish. The Forrests had moved up from Atlanta permanently just a few weeks before. All their possessions were moved up at that time. They'd gathered together a little bit of furniture for their room; it was all burned. Only the records and books for the Institute, which were kept in a large, heavy iron safe in the office, were not destroyed.

Much had been done in the way of improvement on the building. It was getting along in years when purchased and was needing constant repair. Most of those repairs had been made, and the building was in fine shape in every way. Now everything seemed to have been done in vain.

The people of Toccoa, upon seeing the smoke and blaze, drove out from town. Since the Institute had been near Toccoa for only two years, the Forrests and their associates didn't have a great host of personal friends; but everyone was interested in the burning of a big building like that. The townspeople were very kind; they offered clothing, bedding, and food. Many of them opened their homes to students until some kind of provision could be made for caring for them. Everybody wanted to help, yet nobody had any idea that the school would continue—indeed, there was nothing with which to continue. Only Miss Staley's house and the unfinished barn remained.

At the time of the fire Rev. Forrest was in Miami. He had been attending a missionary conference there; at its conclusion he went to the railway station, thankful—as always—that he could turn his steps homeward for a few short days before starting out again. He was standing at the head of the steps, ready to go down and board the train as soon as it was called.

A messenger boy came up the steps just then, carrying a telegram. Rev. Forrest had a hunch. He asked, "For whom is that telegram?"

The boy answered, "Somebody named Forrest."

"I'm the man." Filled with sudden dread, he tore open the envelope, pulled out the telegram, and read: "Institute building burned to ground today. Come home at once." It was from Mrs. Forrest.

His first reaction to the message was wondering why his knees wouldn't hold him up. He wasn't thinking about the fire or the loss. Just wondering what was the matter with his knees, they felt like jelly.

He nearly fell down the steps when his knees buckled under him. He noticed a chair close by and sat down in it for a little bit. When the train was called, he stumbled down to it and got on in a daze. What could he do? How could they go on? They still owed $20,000.00, and now there was nothing left to show for it. Was God displeased? Did He not want the school to continue? How? What? Why?

Finally he went to sleep. In the middle of the night the porter woke him and said, "Somep'n sho is wrong wid you, boss, cap'n, you been teahin' up dis whole cyah." He had an upper berth and was sitting on the edge of it pulling on the curtains and yelling, "Fire! Fire!"

There were a dozen kinds of pajamas and nightshirts running up and down the aisle looking for a fire.

His wife met him at the Toccoa Railway Station. She was driving Nellie, hitched to a buggy. She tried to tell him on the way out home how the fire had occurred. She was very

71

calm and serene about it, although she didn't have a change of clothing, unless it may have been given to her in the meantime. Rev. Forrest wasn't beside himself about the tragedy—he was just paralyzed with fear and wondering what to do. He knew that there were forty-seven students, plus the faculty, waiting for Brother Forrest to get home to tell them the next step. They were staying at the neighboring houses, of which there were very few, or with friends in Toccoa. Some answer—some plan—had to be given them.

When the Forrests drove onto the campus, the students were all gathered at the blackened and still smoking ruins. Everybody had agreed that no one was to cry when Rev. Forrest arrived; but it would have been better if they'd all been weeping, for he could see the efforts to keep straight faces and be cheerful. What a task that was under such circumstances! They sang all the hymns and choruses they knew and tried their best to be courageous and to encourage him. Still he knew not what to say, or how to advise the teachers and staff members. However, he never had for one moment the idea of quitting.

At first some of the faculty, as well as the students, thought: "We can't go on like this. We have nothing with which to continue. What can we do but quit?"

Rev. Forrest refused to harbor a thought like that. "I feel God wants us to continue. There must be some way to do so. How to begin or what to do even to get started I do not know. But God will provide. We cannot quit. Are you with me?"

The students answered that they wouldn't go home if there was any way at all of staying.

Mr. Hubbard, assistant to Rev. Forrest, accepted the challenge with the words: "It's up to you now; I don't see how we can go on, but it's up to you. If you say go on, we'll do it somehow."

72

When the other teachers echoed his words, there was nothing else to do but continue the work.

Miss Staley was a tower of strength. She said, "Of course, Richard, we'll go on. We can't stop. The Lord called us to do this work. There's my house up on the hill. Use it any way you like."

He accepted her invitation: "All right, we'll do our cooking in your kitchen, then, and fix up a dining room in your basement."

For some time the Staley Cottage was the headquarters for the Institute. The floor of the basement was cemented, and within a short time all staff members and students ate their meals there.

For the next two or three days after his decision to remain, Rev. Forrest was in a state of turmoil. He had little peace of mind. One question kept recurring: Was this decision correct? He did not want to quit; he felt that God would not want the school to close—but, oh, if the Lord would only give him a sign! The problems seemed insurmountable; nonetheless, if he *knew* that God was for him, he'd go on—despite any circumstance and any person who might be opposed.

Then in the midst of many questionings, God in His compassion spoke to His dear child, giving him the sign he sought—the verse which has been his unfurled standard throughout the following years. It happened this way:

Rev. Forrest started down the hill from Staley Cottage one morning. His steps led him to the pile of ashes that was all that remained of his dreams. He wandered around, poking about with a stick. Finally he sat down on a rock under where their room had been. He noticed a thin line of smoke still rising and poked at the smouldering embers —they were the remains of his books. He had just purchased a set of Encyclopedia Britannica—those and his other books were still burning. Up to that time he hadn't shed a tear; actually he'd been too paralyzed. Now the sight of the ashes of his books unleashed the floodgates, and he "wept like a girl," he later said. Complete discouragement swept over him.

It was at this moment that God spoke. Clearly His child heard the promise: *To appoint unto them that mourn in Zion, to give unto them beauty for ashes, the oil of joy for mourning, the garment of praise for the spirit of heaviness; that they might be called trees of righteousness, the planting of the Lord, that he might be glorified.* (Isaiah 61:3)

Rev. Forrest knew the first part of the verse, but he couldn't recall even having read the latter part. Yet God revealed it unto him: "that they might be called trees of righteousness, *the planting of the Lord,* that he might be glorified."

"Thank you, Lord," he breathed, "I don't know how we'll do it, but Thou dost."

So saying, he got up, squared his shoulders, and started to town to see the one person most likely to hinder the work —the man from whom Haddock Inn had been purchased and to whom $20,000.00 was still owing.

This man was very prosperous; he owned the bank and the cotton mill (now the Thread Mill) in town and hundreds of acres of land. He also had extreme views on religion. He believed in a second chance after death, annihilation, that the Holy Spirit had no personality, and other doctrines in conflict with those taught at Toccoa Falls Institute. It later seemed evident that he had sold the Inn to Rev. Forrest expecting to be one of the teachers—and was disgruntled because his services had not been sought. Consequently he felt that the Forrests were not competent to run a school—and indeed they wouldn't have been, had they not been led by supernatural guidance.

It was this man whom Rev. Forrest went to see. His first

words to the young man were: "I'd like to have the place back." That meant that he'd keep what had been paid to him during the two years, also.

Rev. Forrest replied, "That's not in my hands. We have a corporation formed and I'd have to consult the other brethren; but I'll tell you now that when I do consult them, I'll advise them to go on with the school. I'm going to volunteer to take the problem upon myself."

Within a few days the Toccoa Falls Institute Corporation met. When Rev. Forrest told the members of the group how he felt, Mr. Lewis simply affirmed: "That suits me." Miss Staley reiterated: "We cannot quit. We must go on." Both stood by and backed his decision.

However, some of his best friends thought that he was utterly foolish and most unwise. Some of the members of the committee felt likewise. Unrest developed even among the faculty. Although they all remained, had it been the first part of the school year instead of near the end, some probably would have quit.

Nor had Rev. Forrest's problems with the former owner ended. Shortly before the fire, the Institute had bought from him sixty acres of land called the Elrod field. (It is a beautiful field across the road from Indian Cemetery.) The school was paying $600.00 twice a year on that property, plus the payments on the original debt.

Mr. Forrest was plowing there with a mule, Mary, when he caught sight of his creditor coming across the field on horse back. The horse was nicely gaited and graceful, and they made a fine picture. The older man cantered up and began a conversation. "Well, I certainly do admire your pluck in going ahead anyhow, and I've decided to go with you, heart and soul."

"Sir, I appreciate that." (These were unusual words. Had the man finally been touched? Was he going to donate some money or cancel out at least part of the indebtedness?

He held a $10,000.00 fire insurance policy on Haddock Inn, taken out before selling it. Would he apply that on what was still owing—and perhaps cancel the rest?)

The man on horseback penetrated his thought and put an end to his hopes with the question: "Now, what day shall I come for my classes?"

"Why, what classes do you mean?"

"My Bible classes."

"Oh," Rev. Forrest hesitated, "that's————different, sir. I thought you were going to be of some financial help to us." (Might as well tell him the truth.)

"No, sir!" Very decisively he spoke. "I want to teach the Bible."

"If you could possibly leave out those things on which we disagree concerning the Bible, that'd be all right; but you can't teach what we consider to be error."

"What do you mean? Do you mean what you say?" he ripped out.

"Yes, sir."

"And you'd have me wear a muzzle?"

"Well, I wouldn't put it that way, but you can't teach those things which we know you believe and which we believe to be erroneous. Far better not to have a Bible school at all than to have taught things that are not correct."

"Well, I declare. You really mean it?" The older man was almost unbelieving; then he delivered his ultimatum. "Let me tell you something, sir. I wash my hands of the whole outfit right now."

As he rode off, his horse kicked up a clod which struck Rev. Forrest on the cheek. Although the man wouldn't have done such a thing deliberately, if he could, yet the incident seemed significant and portentous.

Troubles never come singly, someone has said, and this adage was certainly borne out within the next few days and months.

The next day, Rev. Forrest received a bill for ninety

dollars for electricity. As has been recorded, he had been promised electricity without obligation. This had seemed fair, since the wires from the plant to Toccoa ran right across the campus. This bargain notwithstanding, the Institute had decided to become more independent by building its own little power plant, the ruins of which can still be seen below the lake where Dead Man's Branch enters Toccoa Creek. Rev. Forrest himself was doing most of the construction work, which was far from completed.

The bill for electricity came from the bank. Rev. Forrest, thinking that some clerk there had made a mistake, wrote a letter and told them so. An answer came by return mail, saying they were not mistaken and unless the bill was paid in ten days, the Institute lights would be cut off. No one had the money with which to pay. At the end of ten days the lights went out. For seven months kerosene lamps were burned, until the bill could be settled.

The final shock was in the form of two lawsuits. Rev. Forrest owed sixty dollars to one merchant in Toccoa and sixty-three dollars to another. On the false assumption that the school would get the insurance money, each sued to get his share. There was nothing with which to make settlement. All that Rev. Forrest could do was to promise that he'd pay the accounts in full as soon as possible. Finally the money came, and each account was settled.

To the ordinary man, such a series of blows would be insurmountable. On the other hand, to this man of God *all things are possible*. How could there be "beauty for ashes"? How could the school go on—without a place to live, a place to work, with no classrooms, and above and over all a twenty-thousand dollar debt to pay? Yet God had promised—and He does not fail!

So—bowed, but with unshaken faith—facing defeat, but with the promise "beauty for ashes"—the Forrests made their choice, steadfast in their belief that "though impossible," the school would live and grow, blessed of the Lord.

Chapter Eleven

"And Jesus looking upon them saith, With men it is impossible, but not with God: for with God all things are possible."
MARK 10:27

"AN INSTITUTION such as ours must go through three stages," Dr. Forrest has said, "first, survival; then expansion; and last approval."

In 1913 the battle for survival began in earnest. Because of the $20,000.00 debt on the rubble which had been Haddock Inn, the pioneers of the school actually had to begin below the bottom. With a passionate desire for the preservation of the school and all it meant flaming and glowing in their hearts, the staff and students rallied round their leader. They were beginning a battle to retain the precious heritage for which they had come to Toccoa Falls Institute.

The first and most crucial problem was housing. There was certainly no money with which to rebuild. Furthermore, living quarters must be provided immediately. True, neighbors and friends were at present caring for the forty-seven students; but that couldn't go on indefinitely. The sooner the school could become self-sustaining, the better would its testimony be. In addition, God's name would be more highly exalted.

So Rev. Forrest went on his face in prayer, asking guidance. "How, Lord, can we house our Institute family and provide classroom space?"

God provided the answer. "What about tents?"

Rev. Forrest went to Atlanta, contacted the M. D. Smith

Tent Company, and bought enough tents for staff members, students, classrooms, and offices.

Actually the tents were far more durable and comfortable than most people imagine. Lumber was cheap then, so a double floor was laid in every tent. Also, a wainscoting of lumber about four feet high was erected. Then the tent was tacked down on the outside. The top of each tent was more than head high. A screen was built for the front, with a panel inserted in it for the winter months. A sheet iron stove was placed in each for burning wood during the colder months. Electricity was used for lighting all the tents. Every faculty member had his own tent; there were two or three students in each.

Apparently everyone was happy. It was a novel experience, of course. Not long afterward the Hubbard baby was born in a tent home. For three years the tents were used for classrooms and living quarters. Constantly other students came to enroll in this unique school.

Of these days Dr. Forrest says: "The students kept coming—why, I do not know. Why they stayed, I couldn't tell anybody. We had the sweetest kind of time; nobody complained; everybody was happy.——Then we began slowly to climb."

One of the first objectives was to get the $20,000.00 debt paid. Rev. Forrest felt that he needed to get even with the bottom before he could begin a building program. He has always had a great hatred of debt. Providentially, he was called to California for a meeting shortly after the fire. Through contacts made there, he was able to see the huge obligation wiped out. God touched the heart of Mr. Lyman Stewart to send him a check for $15,000.00; Mr. Milton Stewart, his brother, provided the other $5,000.00. Praise God! *He is faithful that promised.*

One morning after breakfast at Staley Cottage, Rev. Forrest came down to what is now the center of the campus.

With a briar hook and an axe he cleared a spot for a permanent dining room and kitchen. When a large enough space had been obtained, everyone assembled in the opening for prayer. Thereupon—with the Forrests in the lead—faculty, staff, and students marched around the clearing, taking it in the name of the Lord for a dining room.

Then they began to build. The money came one week at a time—no more, no less—until the dining room and kitchen were erected. The students did most of the labor, aided by a friend from Atlanta, Georgia, Mr. Adolphus, who was a builder. He volunteered his services and came up to the Institute to superintend the construction.

At the completion of this building, the tents were moved nearby. Then a board shack—just boards up and down, with battens over the cracks—was put up for housing some of the new girls. The Forrests, too, had a room in the building, which became the headquarters for the school. Chapel and the larger classes were held in the dining room. Miss Staley's classes continued to meet at her cottage.

It was now 1916. While the tents had provided adequate lodging for three years, some were now beginning to deteriorate. The Forrests were concerned that the girls, at least, have better living quarters. It was Mrs. Forrest's privilege to furnish the money for the first step in this direction.

Mrs. Forrest has always been a born teacher. At various conventions and conferences attended by the Forrests, she would soon gather together the children and women and have Bible classes. Her classes were always large, for she could make the Bible live as she taught. The children's groups—called Sunshine Bands—gave their pennies, nickels, and dimes to construct an eight-room frame cottage. In this cottage, named "Sunshine" for the children, the girls were housed until a larger building could be erected for their use.

Early in the twenties two companion cottages were built near Sunshine. Anderson Cottage was financed with annuity money from Mrs. J. W. Anderson (with whom the Forrests had lived in Orlando in 1901). Mrs. Anderson built the house at her own expense; she lived in it as a house-mother and filled it with boys. She was a real Godsend to the campus—a wonderful old lady in many ways—sweet and motherly. She didn't care "a hoot" about girls, but she was a real friend of boys. She mothered them and pled for any boy who got into trouble. They in turn called her "Mother A" and tried to live up to her expectations for them.

Burt Cottage was built by a Mrs. Snow of Durham, North Carolina, in memory of her parents, whose last name was Burt. The principal, Rev. J. W. Philp, lived there.

(Today two of the cottages are used by faculty members; the third is the infirmary building.)

Each of these cottages cost less than two thousand dollars, lumber and labor both being cheap and easily obtainable. Ten cents an hour was the average wage paid for common labor in this section. Rev. Forrest could never give a man only ten cents an hour—his conscience wouldn't allow him to do so. He paid his employees twenty cents an hour—and got twenty cents worth of work.

By 1917 it was obvious that the girls would need a larger dormitory than Sunshine Cottage. Acting on faith, Mr. Forrest set aside a plot of land a short distance south of the dining room and broke ground for a two-story building for girls. There was no money—not even ten dollars—toward the building, nor did he intend to build until the necessary sum had been obtained, for he was extremely cautious about doing anything unless he had the money for it.

The next day after the groundbreaking ceremonies, Rev. Forrest left for Los Angeles to preach at a convention there.

All the way out on the train he was thinking how he wished he could meet a man out there named Stewart—Lyman Stewart—the president of the Union Oil Company and the man who had given $600,000.00 to start the building of the Bible Institute of Los Angeles (BIOLA).

After he arrived, he told his friend George Davis, the pastor at whose church the convention was being held, that he hoped to see Lyman Stewart while out there, for "maybe he can help us some."

"Oh," Rev. Davis replied, "now listen. I wouldn't discourage you for anything, Brother Forrest, but you might just as well dismiss that idea; for you never would get within a mile of Lyman Stewart, particularly if he thought you needed any money. Everybody's hounding him for financial help."

"Well," responded Rev. Forrest, "I have no idea of hounding him, but I'd like to tell him what we're trying to do. Maybe he'd like to help. He can do what I can't do, and I can do over there in Georgia what he can't do—maybe we could get together."

"No, just forget it," was the discouraging answer.

The very next day Rev. Forrest was standing on the corner of Fifth and Hope Streets. He had heard that Dr. R. A. Torrey, President of the Bible Institute of Los Angeles, was preaching somewhere at noon every day that week, it being Passion Week. Since no one around the school seemed to know where he was speaking, Rev. Forrest had wandered out onto the street wondering what to do, since he wanted to hear Dr. Torrey that noon.

While hesitating, he noticed a gentleman coming down the street—a very ordinary-looking old man. Rev. Forrest had only one idea in his mind—where was Dr. Torrey preaching? He had known him before now and wanted to see him and hear him and say hello. On impulse, then, he stopped the old gentleman and said, "Do you live in Los Angeles, sir?"

"Yes, sir, I happen to live here. What can I do for you?"

"Do you happen to know Dr. R. A. Torrey, the president of this Bible school here?"

"Well, yes, I know Dr. Torrey."

"Do you know where he's preaching at noon every day this week?"

"No, sir, I'm sorry.——Wait a minute. I think it's the First Methodist Church. It's right down the street about three blocks. I'm going down that way. Let's walk down together."

"That's fine."

As they passed the Bible Institute, Rev. Forrest said, "My, isn't that a wonderful institution? I understand Dr. Torrey is president of this school."

"Yes, we're very proud of that school here in California."

"I understand it was the munificent gift of one man that made it possible—an old fellow gave $600,000.00 to start it. Isn't it wonderful for an old man to use his money that way for God?"

He said, "Surely is. We're glad he did in this case. You interested in that kind of work?"

"Very much. We have a school like it in embryo over in Georgia."

When the old man began to ply him with questions, Rev. Forrest told him about the fire, about his discouragement, about how the Lord spoke to him about going on with the task. He concluded: "Are you interested in this kind of work?"

"Yes," said the old gentleman, "very much." By this time they had arrived at the church. "Here," he said. "There's the sign. Dr. Torrey's speaking here today. I was right after all."

"Thank you, sir," said Rev. Forrest. "I've thoroughly enjoyed this chance meeting with you. Are you a Christian, sir?"

He stopped abruptly and said, "Yes, sir, I am; but that's

the first time anybody's ever asked me that question; and I'll never forget it, sir."

"Well, sir, I've enjoyed talking with you. Forrest is my name."

"I've enjoyed it, too. Stewart is mine—Lyman Stewart."

Rev. Forrest was so surprised and flabbergasted that he couldn't even say goodby. Here he'd been saying the very things he'd have liked to tell Mr. Stewart if he'd had an audience, but he'd talked without any embarrassment this way. He was dumbfounded.

Mr. Stewart went across the street with his shoulders shaking. At first it looked as though he was choking. After he got to the other curb, he turned around and waved his hand, still chuckling.

The next day Rev. Forrest was scheduled to speak to the students of the Bible School. When he walked into the office, Dr. Torrey greeted him with the challenge: "Say, Forrest, what in the world have you done to Lyman Stewart?"

Rev. Forrest sputtered, "Oh, Dr. Torrey, did I say the wrong thing?"

"Wrong thing nothing! He's raising sand around here. He gave the money to build a Bible school to train young people to do Christian work, and he has to wait for you to come all the way over here from Georgia to ask him if he's a Christian. No, you didn't say the wrong thing, I'll tell you that!"

The next day Rev. Forrest left for home. When he looked in his mailbox before departing, he found an envelope. In it was a check for one thousand dollars from Lyman Stewart. There was no letter—just the check.

On the way east he stopped in Chicago to speak in the Moody Memorial Church. Rev. Paul Rader, a friend of Rev. Forrest, was then the pastor.

Just as the congregation was singing the last hymn before the sermon, Rev. Forrest saw someone coming down the aisle. He leaned over and said, "Paul, I think that's William E. Blackstone. Is it?"

"I declare I believe it is." Rev. Rader dashed down to meet him and bring him up onto the platform.

Rev. Forrest had met Mr. Blackstone on a previous trip to California. He was a lawyer, into whose hands Mr. Lyman Stewart and his brother Milton had recently put two and a half million dollars to be given for Christian work at home and abroad. Part of that money was used to build a magnificent hospital in the middle of China.

Mr. Blackstone came up onto the platform. He wore thick glasses and his eyes looked like buckshot. He spoke in a staccato manner. He said, "Well, I declare. Forrest. Where did you come from? Lyman Stewart told me to look you up when I came east if I had to go all the way to Georgia to find you—and here you're the first man I meet that I know. When can you come to see me?"

Rev. Forrest remembered the two and a half million, and Blackstone knew it. He grinned at the statement: "I'll come anytime, anywhere, any way you say, Mr. Blackstone."

"Meet me at the Moody Institute tomorrow morning at ten o'clock in the superintendent's office."

"I'll be right there, sir."

The first thing Mr. Blackstone said when Rev. Forrest walked in the following morning was, "Well, Forrest, what are you building down there now that needs some money?"

"Everything; but the first thing we're working on now is a dormitory cottage for girls to get them in out of tents, shacks, and crowded quarters."

"How much will it cost?"

"Forty-five hundred dollars, as I estimate, for a two-story frame building."

"I was told to ask what you're doing and how much it would cost, and tell you to go ahead and finish it and we'll pay for it."

Rev. Forrest found out afterward it would have been just the same if he'd said forty-five thousand.

Mr. Stewart became a generous donor to Toccoa Falls Institute. About a year later he sent for Rev. Forrest to come to Los Angeles. Naturally he went, wondering all the while as to the cause of the summons.

One afternoon Mr. and Mrs. Stewart called for him at four o'clock to go riding. As Rev. Forrest got in, he noticed that Mrs. Stewart was driving and that the superintendent of BIOLA was also in the car.

As they rode along, Mr. Stewart turned to Rev. Forrest and said, "We've ganged up on you, Brother Forrest, in this sightseeing trip. We have something up our sleeve. Uncle Tom here is getting along in years; he's our superintendent down at the school, you know. We wondered if you would be interested in coming out here as Uncle Tom's understudy, so that when he goes to heaven you can step into his place as superintendent of BIOLA?"

Almost stunned by the magnitude of the statement, Rev. Forrest could only say, "Mr. Stewart, I don't know what I could say to you. That's a wonderful, wonderful thought you've expressed."

"We've prayed about it and decided to ask you to leave Toccoa Falls and come here."

Rev. Forrest's next statement was characteristic of the man: "I couldn't answer you right off the bat. That's so important a question I couldn't answer it without praying about it and finding what the Lord wants me to do."

Mr. Stewart turned to the superintendent. "Tom, I told you he'd say that." Then he turned back to the younger man. "All right. Let's go riding again tomorrow afternoon at the same time."

"Very well, sir."

The next afternoon they went out again.

"Well, what's the answer?"

"Now, Mr. Stewart, I hope you won't misunderstand me and think I don't appreciate the magnificent suggestion you've made, but I'll tell you. I happened to see a picture last night of Lord Fauntleroy, the little boy dressed up in such fine clothes. In the same magazine next to Little Lord Fauntleroy I saw a street urchin from the slum district. He was in rags, but his mother was there with him. They were asking her which she'd rather have, Little Lord Fauntleroy or this ragged little boy. 'I'll take the ragged little fellow,' she answered, 'because *he* belongs to me—*he's mine!*' That's the best way I can answer you, Mr. Stewart."

He said, "Tom, I told you that's what he would say."

The following day Rev. Forrest was leaving again for Toccoa Falls. Again he found an envelope in his mailbox as he checked out. In the envelope was another check for one thousand dollars, accompanied by a little card on which was written the message—"For the ragged little boy."

After this incident Mr. Stewart continued making generous contributions to Toccoa Falls Institute.

The Ella M. Stewart Dormitory was named in honor of Mrs. Stewart and in recognition of Mr. Lyman Stewart's making the building possible. When the girls moved in, they were thrilled. Everything was so pretty and clean looking. There were white beds and bedspreads to match in all the rooms. How many prayers of thanksgiving went up to God for His goodness and Mr. Stewart's kindnesses!

The boys, too, profited; for with the girls' moving to Stewart, the fellows moved from tents into Sunshine, the overflow later being housed in Anderson, as has been mentioned. At last everyone was under permanent shelter—for the first time since the disastrous fire of 1913.

As the school kept growing, the need for more classrooms

and a larger chapel became increasingly acute. One end of the dining room had been left unfinished with the idea that some day a chapel would be placed there. Now seemed to be the time to break ground for this addition.

Leaving those at home to do two things—pray for money and dig down to solid rock for a foundation for the building, Rev. Forrest went to New York to preach in a large gospel tent in the Bronx. On the first night there he was introduced to a number of people who were helping in the meeting, including a middle-aged German lady who played the piano for the services. The second night he was there, this pianist, Miss C. F. L. Schultz, asked him if he'd walk with her to the car line, as she had something she wanted to speak to him about. "I want to talk to you about something," she kept repeating.

Rev. Forrest had never seen her until the night before. "I suppose she has some spiritual problem," he thought.

They walked in silence up the street. He waited for her to open the subject. Finally she broke the silence: "You know, I can't get you out of my mind. I made some inquiries today about where you live and what you're doing, and I understand you have a school in Georgia."

"That's right."

After walking in silence for a few more minutes, she continued, "The Lord told me to ask you what you're doing right now about rebuilding. I understand you've had a fire."

"Yes, we're rebuilding—we're building a chapel."

"How much will it cost?"

"About four thousand dollars." (This was the minimum cost, counting on student labor. Naturally, he was thinking in terms of a frame building, not daring to hope for anything more elaborate.) "Yes, four thousand dollars," he repeated.

"I was praying for you this morning, and the Lord told me to ask you that question and then give you one-half of whatever amount you said—on condition that you raise the other half somewhere else. If you'll go with me to my apartment, I'll give it to you tonight."

He went with her and got a check for two thousand dollars. With this money the downstairs, or chapel, part of the building was completed. Soon Miss Gertrude Fletcher, one of the Institute teachers, highly gifted as an artist, painted the words of John 3:16 on the center rafter of the room. The following year she completed a beautiful scenic painting on the wall behind the pulpit.

This room was destined to be the scene of many transactions between needy souls and their Maker. Hundreds and hundreds of young folks have found God while kneeling round the altar; many, many others have here yielded their all to Him and answered the call to Christian service, some going to the far ends of the earth—yea, even to persecution, the loss of health, or death—in order that precious souls might be brought into His kingdom.

For nearly two years after the chapel was put into use, the upper story stood unfinished. No flooring covered the rafters. Only the uprights for classroom partitions had been put in place. Still no money came to proceed. Finally the entire Institute family met one day in the chapel for a season of prayer to the end that the necessary two thousand dollars come in. At the conclusion of the prayer meeting, everyone went upstairs. As the group circled about, walking on planks which had been laid down on the rafters, they claimed each classroom for the Lord and for His use.

Within a short time a check came from Mrs. Milton Stewart in California for finishing the classrooms. All rejoiced and went to work. Even Mrs. Forrest, other women teachers, and the girls nailed laths on the walls. At first one or two of the smaller rooms were used for offices; after the Administration Building was constructed, partitions were removed, providing five spacious rooms which are used mainly for college classes.

By 1922 it was evident that the Institute could no longer

get along without a central office building; furthermore, additional dormitory space was needed. At this time Rev. Forrest decided to erect a cement block building, instead of frame, as had heretofore been the case. It is interesting to note that the concrete blocks were poured by the students, one of whom was E. Kelly Barnes, now superintendent of the Institute. All finishing materials as well as the framing for the building came through the school's own saw-mill and planing-mill. The work was done, as was customary, with a small force of men supplemented by the student help. Thus a durable, well-constructed building could be made at a minimum cost.

The Administration Building, or ADM, as it is usually called, was made possible by gifts of $10,000.00 from Mrs. R. W. Belo, a dear old saint from Winston-Salem, North Carolina. Rev. Forrest first became acquainted with her and her husband in Orlando, Florida, where they spent their winters. Captain Belo was a crusty old gentleman, a member of one of the first families of Winston-Salem.

The Belos were very warm friends of the Forrests. One day as they were out riding, Captain Belo asked, "What's the official name of your school?" Mr. Forrest told him. He said, "I just wanted to know."

It was at that time that he put the Institute into his will. As he and his wife had no children, he willed everything he had to Mrs. Belo, should he die first, and with her consent it was to come to the school at her death. She in turn made a supplementary will, just like his. After his death in 1919 she decided to give the money, $10,000.00, to the Institute at once as an annuity. Until her death in 1930 she received fifty dollars a month interest.

Before the Forrests left for their trip to Africa in 1930, Rev. Forrest called on Mrs. Belo to say goodby. At the moment of parting, she smiled sweetly and said, "Brother Forrest, I probably won't be here when you come back, but

90

you know where to find me." She was one of the holiest characters Rev. Forrest ever knew, a very cultured woman of the old southern type, yet sweet and humble—really a friend of the school.

By 1923 the Institute owned 527 acres of land, about half woodland and 160 acres tillable. There was an abundant water supply for personal and Institute use and for electric power. The Institute owned its light plant, saw-mill, planing-mill, steam laundry, canning factory, and broom factory. All these represented convenience, quality, and economy. At this time there were twelve buildings, large and small; so, for the first time since the holocaust of 1913, the physical equipment was adequate. God had abundantly supplied.

As Rev. Forrest reviewed the decade from 1913 to 1923, as he walked about the campus, as he read letters from former students now scattered to the ends of the earth—his heart was filled with a paean of praise. "Truly God is 'able to do exceeding abundantly above all that we ask or think,'" he meditated. "We surely have 'beauty for ashes, the oil of joy for mourning, and the garment of praise for the spirit of heaviness.' Praise His holy name!"

He squared his shoulders as he looked toward the future, secure in the promise of Philippians 1:6—*Being confident of this very thing, that he which hath begun a good work in you will perform it until the day of Jesus Christ.*

Chapter Twelve

"And the things that thou hast heard of me among many witnesses, the same commit thou to faithful men, who shall be able to teach others also."—II TIMOTHY 2:2

"OF ALL UNDEVELOPED resources, human souls and minds offer the greatest possibilities. There are hundreds of consecrated young people who are eager for such training. Every one who gets it and goes out to work for the Master starts a multiplication table of blessing that will never stop growing until Jesus comes."

This statement, copied from an early school bulletin, was written by Mr. Forrest. It furnishes the keynote of his Christian philosophy: Find young people, get them saved, train them, send them out so that they may in turn win others to Christ and teach the Christian way of life.

Students during the early years came not only from the South, but from such far away places as Pennsylvania, Ohio, and New York. They started coming from these states, then went home and became advertisers to others. Students were enrolled from wealthy homes and log cabins. They were a fine loyal group, bound together by a vision of taking Christ to all the world. Some would be missionaries to far-off lands; others would preach or teach the Word at home; all were led by visions bright and beautiful to a unique place of preparation—Toccoa Falls Institute.

The student family was a happy one. Through and over all the material things—and many times in spite of lack of them—a warm, rich, wholesome spiritual atmosphere prevailed. Habits of prayer and private devotions were taught. Every effort was made to have the young people grounded and settled in their own spiritual lives. Each knew that he or she always had ready access to any of the teachers for spiritual help or counsel. Because the students were housed in smaller buildings, there grew a happy home or family feeling instead of mere institutional life. School rules and regulations were few and only such as seemed best for all, and they were obeyed cheerfully.

School life furnished many opportunities for practical or vocational training. Students were taught farming, caring for stock, cutting and sawing timber, carpentry, making cement blocks, gardening, laundering, cooking, baking, canning fruits and vegetables, sewing, office work, and the like. (The school has always functioned on the principle that students are better educated if they can perform certain practical tasks; therefore, each person enrolled is expected to work a certain number of hours per week under a Work Training Program. The results have been two-fold: training for those participating, and a cutting down of the expenses of running the Institute.)

Life at Toccoa Falls was not all work, however. Opportunity was given for wholesome, healthful recreation. There were hiking, swimming, tennis, basketball, and baseball— to mention only a few diversions. Music, for both service and recreation, was stressed.

Despite problems and difficulties that would arise from lack of home training, the Forrests continued to take in needy young people, so long as they had a conscious knowledge of salvation and a heart and life yielded to God for service. How could Rev. Forrest refuse appeals like the following:

Dear Sir:—I am thinking of going to school and i think i wood like to come down to you school my sister told me that was a fine school and i sure think so

and I am moore anioux to come sence she has told
about the school Please Write and send me a blank if
thir will be any room and work for me and i will enter
In as school openes

You verry truely

Gentlemen:—As a friend I will write to you concerning your school, I am a boy who would like to have
such training as your school gives. I am an average
boy with little money to go to school on, and beg that
you send me a catalog and the plans by which I could
get into your school. I would like to work my way
please let me know at once, when school opens, etc.

Yours truly

Although letters as poorly written as the first one quoted
were rare, even in the early days, yet, with the proper
training and education, these young people made good
students and fruitful workers. What a joy it was to take
them as rough nuggets and polish them until the gold
shone forth!

Practical Christian living was taught, not only in the
classroom, but also in living example as the Forrests and
the faculty members evidenced it day by day. An enthusiastic boy named Willie, now a successful preacher in Pennsylvania, was the recipient of a lesson depicting absolute
dependence upon God, on one occasion.

At that time the Forrests had many boxes and barrels of
used clothing which was sent to them by friends. They
had even built a shack for use as a storehouse. Time and
time again—it was the ordinary course of events—the mountain people would come and find clothes there that fitted
as though they'd been made for them. The Forrests would
sell the garments for a shadow of what they were worth;
but what they got was all clear, and the folks who bought
were happy about the transaction, too.

One day the Forrests were standing near the shack. Willie, whose task it was to drive the horse and make the trips to town for groceries and other necessities, drove up. He got out of the wagon and walked over to Mr. Forrest to ask for the money needed for the groceries. "Here's the list the kitchen gave me," he said, "and they can't get the next meal till I get back with the things, so I guess I'd better be going."

Mr. Forrest answered, "Willie, you'll have to wait until some money comes. We don't have any."

"How's it coming?"

"I don't know, but you'll have to wait. We have to have the money, and we don't have it. We'll just have to wait until the Lord sends it."

While they were still talking, Mr. Forrest saw three men coming up the hill from the county road nearby. He greeted them and found out that they were a father and two sons who had walked over from South Carolina. They said, "We heerd tell you-all got some clothes here that you sell."

Mr. Forrest quickly answered, "Yes, sir, we have some."

Mrs. Forrest entered the conversation. "Yes, sir, come with me; I'll show you what we have."

"Thank you, ma'am," they drawled, and followed her over to the shack where the clothes were hanging. They found suits that fitted perfectly. All three bought suits, shirts, and all kinds of things. Furthermore, they paid cash—twice as much as the groceries would cost.

After the men had paid for the clothes and left, Mr. Forrest called Willie to him. "Come on," he said, "it's time to go to town now."

Such incidents occurred again and again. Was it any wonder that the students learned to trust God, to praise Him, and to love Him? Was it not the normal thing for them to take their problems to Him, to depend on Him, to put their full confidence in Him? With such a living example continuously before them, how could they do otherwise?

Many of the students reached heights for God, even while attending the Institute. The following is a typical example:

Shortly after Haddock Inn was destroyed, a Miss Santley came from Demorest, Georgia, to see about enrolling in school a boy in whom she was deeply interested. He wanted to enter the ministry, but had had very few, if any, privileges for education. His parents were typical mountain folks—honorable, straight-forward people. His mother especially was a very fine Christian woman. Rev. Forrest told Miss Santley to send the boy on, and in a few days he arrived. He said he had just "stepped over," but the "step" was about fifteen miles. The boy, John Brock, was registered as a student and put into one of the tents. A teenager when he came, John took both his elementary and high school training at Toccoa Falls, and then had some Institute work. During this time he met Miss Emma Kimel, who was a student from Winston-Salem. Although "courting" was not allowed in those days, sometimes Mrs. Forrest circumvented the rule by inviting them up to Staley Cottage on Sunday afternoons.

While John was in school, a very great need arose at one time. A special meeting was called in the dining room, and all gathered for prayer. Three hundred dollars was the sum needed—and even one hundred dollars meant a great deal then. After one or two had prayed that God send in the money, John Brock began to pray. It was very unusual for him because he was not very emotional, but he prayed with such a passion and earnestness that it seemed as though he couldn't stop. Everyone in the room was with him; he carried everybody with a passion of prayer to the very throne of God.

Two or three days later Rev. Forrest received a letter

from Richmond, Virginia, from a man whose wife's parents, very godly people, were warm friends of the Forrests. Rev. Forrest was rather surprised to hear from the younger man, as he knew him only casually. The contents of the letter surprised him even more. The man wrote: "I just went over to see the old folks today. While waiting for them to come down, I saw a letter on the table to them from you. Maybe I shouldn't have read it, but I just wanted to see what you were telling them, and I opened the letter, read it, and noticed that you were in need of some help. I hope I'm not just butting in where I'm not wanted; I didn't say anything to the old folks about it, but I felt I should send that help to you." Although the amount needed had not been specified in the letter he'd read, the younger man sent a check for the exact amount for which John Brock and the others had been praying!

A point to be noted is that the man's visit with his wife's parents took place at exactly the same time that John Brock was crying to God in the dining room down in Georgia. Surely John touched God and God touched that man, the superintendent of a prominent seed company in Richmond. That was a direct answer to the prayer of a sincere and consecrated student.

Later John and Emma married and went to Winston-Salem, where he became a Baptist preacher. When their family came, the church was too small to support them, so John added to his income by serving on the police force on week-days, still preaching on Sunday. One day Rev. Forrest was driving through and recognized John as he was directing traffic. He drove up alongside and called, "Listen, officer, can you please tell me the way to go?"

John smiled broadly as he saw who was calling to him. He responded, "I reckon I could, because you told me the same thing. You told me the way to go a good many years ago."

Eleven years ago he moved back to Toccoa Falls to put

his two youngest children in school and to help in the dairy and with truck gardening. In due time those children finished school. One is now serving her second term in the Anglo-Egyptian Sudan in Africa.

Always zealous for the Lord's work, Rev. Brock noticed that there was a group of people living nearby who had no church facilities. He gathered these country folks together and started a church for them in the Toccoa Falls County School. Since then they have built a fine frame church of their own, the Toccoa Creek Baptist Church, on the highway at the edge of the Institute property.

The Forrests were not privileged to have children of their own. Perhaps the Lord felt that theirs was to be a larger ministry than would have been possible with a family to rear. Their home, however, has always been open to young folks. Five of these were given special places and became "their" children.

Ora Frost was the first to come, from the coal mining region of southwest Virginia. The Forrests took her under their wing and provided her education. She is now a successful elementary teacher in Gainesville, Georgia, with a Master's degree from the University of Georgia.

Kelly Barnes and Alice Larson came in 1917, he from Lumberton, North Carolina, and she from Santa Rosa, California. Both of them have always lived with the Forrests. After their training at Toccoa Falls and at Wheaton College, they married and have since been associated with Toccoa Falls Institute as part of the staff. Mr. Barnes is superintendent; Mrs. Barnes, one of the teachers.

Sue Ralls (Mathes) is from Tiptop, Tennessee. Rev. Forrest met her when he was conducting meetings there. He stayed at the Ralls home. There he watched Susie. There was an old Estey parlor organ in the house. Some of the keys would stick, and one pedal was broken. But Susie, who was a chubby little girl, would sit at that organ, furiously work that one good pedal, and play "Nearer, My God, to Thee" and other pieces, simply enrapt. Three years later she came to the Falls. The Forrests took special pains about her musical education; they sent her to the conservatory in Atlanta for a time, then to the conservatory at Brenau College in Gainesville. She later married the business manager of Toccoa Falls Institute and, with the exception of a few years in Florida, has been the head of the music department at Toccoa Falls.

The fifth child, Gladys, was brought to the Forrests by a woman Holiness preacher. She was nine or ten at the time, with light blond hair and deep dark eyes. The Forrests legally adopted her. She later married Paul Gordon, one of the graduating students. Since that time her son Richard has also graduated from the Institute. Both the husband and son are pastors of fine churches in the Chicago area.

On December 7, 1917, the Honorable William Jennings Bryan penned the following note to Rev. Forrest:

> "I commend most cordially the Toccoa Falls Institute. The Bible has a growing place in our educational system. I was much impressed by the spirit of your Institute and the personnel of its teachers, and the work in which it is engaged."

On the following day Dr. M. Ashbey Jones, pastor of the Ponce De Leon Avenue Baptist Church of Atlanta, wrote:

> "I simply want to express to you something of the joy and inspiration I received in my visit to Toccoa Falls Institute last week. Your shops, farm and school rooms are training hands and brains, and the Christian idealism of your entire institution is furnishing a spiritual atmosphere in which the character can only come to maturity. I pray God's richest blessings upon your work in the future."

Someone has said, "The success and development of a school largely depends upon the call and the vision of the founders, the school's traditions, and the character and calibre of its faculty."

Surely this statement is true of Toccoa Falls. Young people go out, grounded in the faith, influencing others for good, because of the kind of instruction that they have had and because of the spirit of sacrifice evident in the lives of the founders and their corps of helpers.

Rev. Forrest by this time was being paid fifty dollars a month as a district superintendent of The Christian and Missionary Alliance. Every cent of this not actually used in his work as superintendent was put into the school. Consequently, there was little money with which to buy clothes.

Mrs. Forrest would dress out of the boxes and barrels of second-hand clothes that were sent in. She was a good seamstress, and her vigor was unbelievable. She could do more work than any other two women on the place. She'd turn those old clothes inside out and upside down and make them all over again. They always looked like new. It hurt Rev. Forrest to see her doing it, though, as he felt that he wasn't properly taking care of her. At the same time he, too, was dressing out of the same boxes and barrels. His tuxedo was obtained that way.

In those days the stipend that the staff and faculty workers got was a mere trifle. Time and again certain of the instructors would stand in Rev. Forrest's office and tear their checks in half and lay the pieces down on his desk. Many times they were really in need; yet they felt the need of the work was greater.

Could the school do other than succeed, with such a heritage? The spirit of prayer and sacrifice was so breathed into the school that anyone coming onto the campus could feel it in the atmosphere. The Reverend Paul Rader, nationally known Christian and evangelist, felt it. After a visit to the Institute, he gave the following testimony:

"Look at what I have found! 'A light under a bushel.' I found it away down in the hills of Georgia.

"I found something that took a girl from the humblest country environment, equipped her, fired her soul and sent her forth to the world fully prepared to be a leader.

"I found this same something dug out and prepared those fine fellows who took gospel tents and put them in neglected spots of the South and preached to many thousands of people, and had hundreds of converts last summer.

"This wonderful 'something' is the Bible School known as the TOCCOA FALLS INSTITUTE, at Toccoa, Ga.

"The school has a wide field (since it is the only one of its character in the southeast), and meets a great need. It is doing a wonderful work, in a great way.

"It fires my soul."

Chapter Thirteen

*'The steps of a good man are ordered by the Lord:
and he delighteth in his way."*—PSALM 37:23

IT IS A BREATH-TAKING experience to place oneself completely
at the disposal of God. No one can foresee through what
vicissitudes he might be led, what heights he may gain,
what victories may be his. Unaided by man, he might be
called upon to charge the citadel of the enemy—or go forward in the strength of the Lord, working out miracles
unbelievable!

Had anyone pushed aside the veil of the future for the
Forrests when they were considering the establishment of
a Bible training school and shown them the stupendous
task they were about to assume, perhaps their hearts would
have failed them for fear. Nonetheless, they would have
set their faces steadily forward, knowing that they were
proceeding with the direction of, and in the strength of, the
Lord.

The establishment of a Bible school is not a thing to be
lightly considered—even with the financial and moral back-
ing of a denomination. To begin and to operate a non-
sectarian Bible institute is inconceivable to the average man.
Yet this became the dream and the achievement of the
Forrests.

The Toccoa Falls Institute was the first non-sectarian
Bible training school in the southeast. Since its aim was
that of aiding needy young folks to get a Christian education, Rev. Forrest felt that the school should be broader
than a single denomination. Therefore, young people with

varied denominational backgrounds have always felt welcome.

Naturally, with Rev. Forrest's close connection with The Christian and Missionary Alliance, there would exist sympathetic relationships between the school and this church group. In fact, for the first few months the school was controlled by The Christian and Missionary Alliance Board of New York. After a short time the Toccoa Falls Institute was incorporated and the charter transferred to the school itself. Since the laws of Georgia forbid a foreign corporation to control the affairs of a non-profit corporation operating in the state, the school has continued through the years as an independent organization, welcoming students from many denominations. The Toccoa Falls Institute does have an affiliated relationship to The Christian and Missionary Alliance, as its faith and teachings are in accord with those of the Alliance, it is recognized as the official school for the Alliance in the southern states, and (since 1950) its students can go directly from the school to the foreign mission field without having to take further training in the Alliance school at Nyack, New York.

Shortly after the inception of the school, Dr. A. B. Simpson came to visit. Rev. Forrest took him up the wooded path to the point where he could first behold the breath-taking beauty of Toccoa Falls. Dr. Simpson stood for a long time looking at the water as it broke into sparkling globules and fell to the pool nearly two hundred feet below; then suddenly he turned and said, "Brother Forrest, thank God for something for which you need not to apologize. This is wonderful." Before he left, he handed Rev. Forrest one thousand dollars of his own money—"Just to encourage you. I believe you're on the right track, and doing the right thing." That was of immense encouragement to the young man as he was starting out in this new field of endeavor.

Dr. Simpson, recognizing the younger man's ability as a preacher, also used him as his supply pastor in the Gospel Tabernacle of New York for about five years. It was during this time that the Forrest Bible Class, a men's class which has had a marvelous ministry, was organized. Young men with cards would stand on the corners two or three blocks around that busy Times Square section. When they saw a man who looked as though he were going no place in particular, they'd approach him, hand him a card of invitation, and say, "Won't you come up to our Sunday-school class? It's meeting upstairs here." Before the hour of the class, Mrs. Forrest would fill a tin bucket with lemonade and put a piece of ice in it. The bucket, with two or three dippers, was placed at the entrance to the classroom. As the men came upstairs, they were told they could take off their coats, loosen their collars if they wished, and have a dipper of ice cold lemonade. Soon eighty to one hundred men were attending that Bible class on Sunday afternoons. The class still continues to meet.

In 1906 Rev. Forrest was first elected as a member of the Board of Managers of The Christian and Missionary Alliance, on which board he has served most of the time since then. While this group was discussing the site for National Council in 1919, Rev. Forrest popped up and said, "Why not bring it to Toccoa Falls?"

The men asked, "Could you take care of us?"

Nonchalantly he replied, "Of course. I don't know how, but we'll take care of you some way." At the time he didn't realize how great the undertaking would be.

As the time for the meeting neared, Rev. Forrest was informed that there would be probably four hundred or more delegates coming from all over the United States. How could they be accommodated? There were only two or three dormitory cottages on the campus—and they were filled with students. A number of the boys were still living in tents.

Rev. Forrest really felt "up against it." What a rash promise to make—to entertain four hundred people with absolutely no place to do so! Finally, while looking at the fellows dashing out of their tents to class, he got an idea. In desperation he went down to Camp Gordon near Atlanta.

General Fitz-hugh Lee, commander of Camp Gordon, greeted him and asked his business.

"I've come to you because I'm in a jam up at Toccoa Falls," was the reply.

"Sit down and tell me about it."

"It's like this. We're supposed to entertain a missionary conference up at Toccoa Falls where we have a little school; and we don't have the accommodations to take care of the number of delegates that are coming, so I wondered if the army could help us out."

"A what!?" ejaculated General Lee.

"A missionary conference," replied Rev. Forrest, with a twinkle in his eye. Despite the serious aspect of the situation, the astonishment of the general was amusing.

"Well," replied the general, "I'll be dogged! That's the first time I ever heard anyone ask the army to entertain a missionary conference. What can we do for you?"

"You can lend me enough tents to take care of about four hundred people, and cots, blankets, and things of that sort."

Again he said, "I'll be dogged!" And then, "We'll do it!"

"Thank you, sir," said Rev. Forrest.

"What are the dates?"

Rev. Forrest told him.

When the time of Council approached, Rev. Forrest began to wonder how he would get the tents and supplies transported to Toccoa Falls. Before he had reached a solution, General Lee sent the equipment to the Institute in a fleet of government trucks. He also ordered a squad of enlisted men along to erect the tents. The soldiers were at the school for several days, pitching the tents wherever they were asked to, setting up the cots, and fixing everything up in just the nicest kind of way. Two of the men were won to Christ during this time.

The date for Council was early in May. After the members had all arrived, the weather turned bitterly cold. General Lee, remembering that the army was in a sense "host" to a missionary conference, sent another consignment of blankets. Rev. Forrest felt fortunate indeed to be in touch with an almost unlimited supply.

Everybody who came to Council was happy and pleased with the novelty of camping out. Everyone had a good time.

The Southern Railway was holding a safety meeting at the same time as Council; the two groups decided to exchange speakers. This created a very fine contact with the Southern Railroad, which has since been very kind to Dr. Forrest and the Institute.

After this, Rev. Forrest went with the superintendent of the Southern Railway in his private car attending safety meetings all up and down the line. He'd speak to the men on religious subjects in between the talks on safety. In that way he became acquainted with a great many of the officials, as well as with a large number of the men who would gather at the given terminal points for these safety meetings.

Incidents like those just mentioned undoubtedly furnish the clue to one of the major reasons why Toccoa Falls Institute has continued to function and grow. Rev. Forrest's way of making friends—not alone in religious circles—but in the business world, in the military field, among the common people—has been of inestimable value to the school of his founding.

In an institute like this, each contact made with an interested person becomes an aid to its survival. By inviting four hundred people from all over the United States to Toccoa Falls for a conference, Rev. Forrest made many people aware of the school's existence; by entertaining this convention in an *unconventional* manner, he publicized the school; by asking the army for help, he made friends in another realm of life; by cooperating with the railroad, he placed the foundation for a friendship that has existed through the years.

Because of the MAN, the school has benefited—in survival, in growth, in acceptance. The contacts he has made have resulted in prayer partners and in contributors, both vital to a non-sectarian school—established in faith, operated in faith, pressing forward in faith!

Chapter Fourteen

*"Enlarge the place of thy tent, and let them stretch forth
the curtains of thine habitations: spare not, lengthen thy
cords, and strengthen thy stakes."*—Isaiah 54:2

"First, survival; then, expansion."

Nineteen Hundred Twenty-three came, and twelve years
had passed; Toccoa Falls Institute had been established—
and had survived against great odds—with its leaders following Jesus each step of the way.

As the first years were characterized by the construction
of a number of small buildings to take the place of the
beautiful inn destroyed by fire, so were the following years
distinguished by activity, albeit of a rather different nature.
While there was some actual building carried on, the greater
emphasis was on expansion in the types of services rendered
by both the founders and the students of the Institute.

From their earliest days at Toccoa Falls, the Forrests
yearned toward the people who lived in the neighboring
hills. It was their earnest desire to become friends with
these neighbors and to help them in any way that they
could.

Mrs. Forrest soon realized that there was no school
nearby and that the children of these families were growing
up without educational opportunities. Though there had
been a school house, called Soapstone School, about a mile
northeast of the campus, it had closed because there were
no teachers. Seeing the need, Mrs. Forrest determined to
start a school for the youngsters. About 1914 she gathered
a number of children together in an old shack—a shanty-like

structure with boards up and down, battens over the cracks, no lining at all, and a great big wood stove for heat. Here she began classes for the elementary grades. She got no pay for her work; at first the county didn't even help fix up the building for use. However, some years later, the county assumed responsibility for the Toccoa Falls Grammar School. A nice brick building on the same site now houses the school and three teachers.

From time to time there came a few opportunities to be of real blessing. A Sunday school was established on the campus for the neighborhood children, and occasional visits were paid to the friends who lived near. These chances to witness seemed dwarfed, however, in comparison to the desire of the Institute young people to be used of the Lord. They felt it a great privilege to come together to study God's Word and to equip themselves for service at home or abroad. Even during their period of study, they wished to spread the good news to others.

At first their work was largely limited to prayer. Later a small number of students were asked to help in the Sunday schools of Toccoa and Stephens County, others witnessed for God in meetings held occasionally on street corners of nearby towns, and some went into homes to comfort in times of sickness or death.

In the fall of 1923 this work was greatly expanded by the establishment of an organized Extension Work Department, by means of which the work mentioned above was carried out more systematically and regularly. In the fall term of 1925-26, for instance, 3,406 were taught in Bible classes; 106 gospel services were held with 36 students and 12 members of the faculty sharing in the extension work; tracts, Gospels, and Testaments were widely distributed; a Moody Colportage Library was placed in a convict camp nearby; and fifty-one persons were led to accept Jesus Christ as their Saviour.

Some years later the young men and the young women of

the Institute formed the Ministerial Association and the Christian Service League, respectively. These organizations continue to function today and carry on the traditions set up early in the history of the school.

Very early in the twenties Rev. Forrest had a visitor from Cuba, Rev. B. G. Lavistida, who was a Presbyterian Cuban missionary. His wife was from New England, where some time before she had met Rev. Forrest. They wanted their boy to attend school in the states, and Rev. Lavistida had come to Toccoa Falls Institute to see about his enrollment. The acceptance of this lad as a student opened the doors of the school to another group of people, the Cubans. At that time Rev. Lavistida, who is the head of a school now at Placetas, Cuba, began sending more students to the Institute —then, as they went back home, they recruited others. Miss Mabel Bailey (now Mrs. Thomas Willey), a graduate of Toccoa Falls, was called to Pinar del Rio as a missionary; she, too, sent Cuban students to the school. So has this phase of the work grown, and through it many souls have been brought to Christ both at Toccoa Falls and in Cuba.

One student, F. Garcia, upon his return to Cuba, summarized the influence of the Institute in a letter to Mr. Forrest:

"I wonder if to say that—I remember TFI—would be the right term to use. I rather would say that—I feel TFI—and am very glad it is so. By TFI I mean the whole thing, or rather, the whole blessing. Beginning with the consecrated people there, and ending with the trees on the campus. The results of my twenty-six months among you are to be felt in my life as long as I live." (Mr. Garcia afterward became pastor of the First Presbyterian Church of Havana, a great church.)

During these years the Toccoa Falls Institute opened its grounds to summer camps. Delegates from many denominations—including Baptist, Christian, Presbyterian, Episcopalian, and The Christian and Missionary Alliance—came together for a season of refreshing and inspiration in this hallowed place. Some of these camps and conferences still continue.

The knowledge and influence of Toccoa Falls Institute was reaching into the far corners of the United States—and beyond. During the school year of 1921-22, students came to Toccoa Falls from twenty-six states, from Iceland, and from Cuba. Their average age was twenty-one.

Because there were more applications than dormitory accommodations for the fall term of 1922, tents were again erected and used by some of the young men for several years. In 1924 a friend of the school erected another building, which was known as the Industrial Building and included the laundry, linen storeroom, and dormitory facilities for some of the staff workers and students. Three years later this building, as well as the cannery nearby, was wiped out by fire. The laundry and canning plant were rebuilt the next year, and both made modern in their equipment. By September, 1928, there were on the shelves nearly 1,300 gallons of canned goods, to be used in the dining room throughout the coming winter. In this way, and in many others, the Institute has always attempted to function as economically as possible.

During these years, also, a step in expansion was taken in the course of study offered. Heretofore, elementary and high school subjects had been taught only to older students who, for some reason, had not been able to attend school during their earlier years. Now it was deemed advisable to institute a complete high school course of study. Accordingly, a Christian high school for younger students—as well as the older ones—was set up in 1928 and fully accredited under the State of Georgia in February, 1929. From that time to the present the students in this course have been taught Christian principles along with secular education. Dr. Forrest has often said that he would rather see a student soundly saved than thoroughly educated—if he could not be both. Praise God! At Toccoa Falls he receives training in both phases of life. Here is the place "Where Christian Character Is Developed With Intellect."

It is a known fact that the personality of Dr. Forrest in his contacts with people all over the world has made Toccoa Falls what it is today. Doors were now opening to him whereby his influence would be felt among several other groups of people.

In November, 1923, the United States Government granted Toccoa Falls a post office and named Rev. Forrest the postmaster. He actively participated in this organization, and has always been welcomed at their conventions, many times being invited as a featured speaker.

Throughout the years Rev. Forrest has been sought after as an evangelist. His contacts on trips throughout the nation (he has preached in all but two states) have made Christ known to countless numbers of souls, have brought faculty members and students to Toccoa Falls, and have won contributors and prayer warriors as "partners" in the enterprise. He has not known denominational barriers. Even in Toccoa he has preached in the various churches. In 1925 the First Presbyterian Church issued him a call to become their pastor. After much consideration and with the understanding that he would be able to continue his evangelistic work throughout the United States and Canada, he accepted the call and served as pastor of this church for twenty-five years. During his pastorate a beautiful brick edifice was built, and the church membership increased. It is of interest to note that, though he felt several times that he should resign because of the pressure of his other duties, the church refused to allow this until he reached the age of retiral.

The uniqueness of the man is evidenced in the fact that

he served as Moderator of the Athens Presbytery and on various other Presbyterian committees—at the same time being a member of the Board of Managers of The Christian and Missionary Alliance and of a number of their committees of national importance. He has helped to examine many young men of both denominations for ordination to the ministry. When he traveled abroad, he visited both the Presbyterian and Alliance mission stations in many countries, representing both foreign mission boards while on his travels.

In 1927 another sphere of activity opened for Rev. Forrest and for the Toccoa Falls Institute, as they undertook the building and operation of Radio Station WTFI. Studios were in the basement of the First Presbyterian Church in Toccoa, and the Sunday morning services were broadcast. The Sunday morning listeners were organized into a large Bible Class, numbering over fifteen hundred. Nearly a thousand of these folks gathered at the Falls for a picnic one fine day, with motor caravans coming from such distant points as Athens, sixty miles away. Mrs. Forrest conducted a weekly Bible study over the air on Thursday evenings.

Rev. Forrest was in the railroad station one day when an old lady who lived away back in the country approached and said, "We-all have been hearin' you preach the Gospel on the air. You don't know me, but a friend said to me, 'This is the man that preaches on the air,' and I wanted to come and tell you how much good it has done me and my family." Such statements have been duplicated hundreds and hundreds of times in letters and postcards and by personal contact.

Several years later the station was sold to the Bulova Watch Company and moved to Atlanta. It is now known as WAGA. Since that time Dr. Forrest has continued his gospel ministry over Radio Station WLET of Toccoa. His Sunday evening messages while pastor of the First Presbyterian Church were broadcast; he continues his "Church of the Wildwood" program each Sunday morning. He is fond of telling of the colored friend who stopped him on the street one day. "Ah wants you to meet you-all's namesake," she said, pulling a little fellow out from behind her skirts. "At fust Ah wuz gonna call him Wildwood, but Ah finally decided on Forrest."

As the school was characterized by its expansion of services and growth in the years from 1923 to 1930, so was this expansion to continue during the years to come. As Rev. Forrest's warm personality and sincere love for people was evidenced through his varied activities of this period, so was he to continue to be a blessing to a great many folks throughout the world. Many problems were to arise, but *no good thing will he withhold from them that walk uprightly.* There were blessings and honors also to come.

Chapter Fifteen

"Blessed be the Lord, who daily loadeth us with benefits."
—PSALM 68:19

IT HAS NEVER been the policy of the leaders of Toccoa Falls Institute to beg for money. Indeed, on many occasions the need has never even been voiced to man. Rather has the admonition of Paul to the Philippians been followed: *In every thing by prayer and supplication with thanksgiving let your requests be made known unto God.* And God has been pleased to answer His children's requests—sometimes in the most unusual ways or from the most unexpected source.

Shortly after the fire that destroyed Haddock Inn, God gave a touching sign that He was mindful of the distress of His servants and that He would restore unto them that which they had lost.

Rev. Forrest had a dear friend in Alabama, a hard-working German farmer. He wrote this friend, Mr. Karl Woerner, telling him about the fire and asking him to pray for wisdom for them, that they might know what to do in replacing the building and carrying on the school.

When the letter arrived, Mr. Woerner and his wife were greatly disturbed about it; that night in their family devotions they prayed very earnestly for Brother Forrest and for the school at Toccoa Falls, that they might have a new building to take the place of the one that had burned.

The children went to bed. After a little while two of

the small sons of the family, Fred and Gustave, came back down stairs. Hesitantly they began, "Papa, you know about our new bicycle?"

Of course he did. For a long time the youngsters had been saving their pennies and nickels and dimes with which to buy a bicycle. They now had fifty dollars and were just waiting for the week end to come when they'd go to market to purchase it.

"Papa, we want to do something about Brother Forrest and the Toccoa Falls school. We've talked it over and we want to send our fifty dollars to him to help build a new building."

"What about your bicycle, boys?"

"We'll start over to save our money for a bicycle."

Mr. Woerner sent the fifty dollars. Rev. Forrest felt as though it was sacred money.

There is a sequel to this act of love. There is a definite promise in the Word of God that He will restore unto us a hundredfold for what we do for Him. Surely this has been the case. After Gustave Woerner and his wife served more than twenty years as missionaries to South China and Borneo, they became members of the staff of Toccoa Falls Institute. In addition, their three lovely children received both their high school and college training at Toccoa Falls; and in turn have all answered the call to the mission field. Several of Fred's children are also graduates of the school.

Over and over again, God has vividly illustrated the value of prayer, as well as His ability to supply any given need in a totally unexpected way.

Rev. Forrest was given definite proof, time after time, of the truth of Cowper's statement: "God works in a mysterious way His wonders to perform." Once, in the early days of the Institute, when the Forrests were total strangers in the community, there arose a need for one hundred dollars with which to pay a note at the bank. Knowing that everyone was afraid to trust them, they felt keenly the importance of making good on every obligation in order to establish a good reputation for the school. At first there was no great concern, for there were several reasons why they had the right to think they would have the money in time to meet the payment; however, as the day approached, for some reason or other all the resources upon which they were depending fell through. They became much concerned; one hundred dollars is not much money, but in those days it meant a great deal.

Rev. Forrest had occasion, just before the note fell due, to go to Atlanta. He thought, "Well, while I'm in Atlanta, somebody will mention money and will come to our help." But nobody did. For some reason he had no supper that evening, and when breakfast time came the next morning he decided to fast through that meal praying for the one hundred dollars.

At eleven o'clock that morning he boarded a train for Toccoa, just to go to the bank and state frankly that he did not have the money and would have to wait a little while before paying it. He had a seat in the day coach next to the dining car. As people went into the diner, Rev. Forrest could smell the food being prepared for lunch. Having had neither supper nor breakfast, he felt so famished that he decided he couldn't wait until he got to Toccoa for his own lunch.

As he was leaving the diner after eating, he passed a table at which was seated a very sweet-faced old lady. To his surprise, she bowed and smiled and called him by name. He thought, "Now I wonder who that could be," at the same time stopping and telling her that he was glad to see her but could not remember her name.

"Oh," she said, "you wouldn't remember me, but I have been greatly blessed under your preaching in New York City. I have been to California and now am on my way back home to New York. When they told me this morning that we were in the state of Georgia, you, of course, came to my mind; and I remembered that you had a school somewhere in Georgia. I was so happy when I saw you come into the dining car a few minutes ago, and I believe the Lord sent you in. I have wanted for a long time to do something to help in the work of the school, but I kept forgetting your address; and when I could have found it, I postponed writing you. Perhaps I could do something to help right now."

Rev. Forrest could have fallen upon her neck, but he didn't. He only said, "Well, you know that help is needed at any time and all the time for a work like the Toccoa Falls Institute."

"Yes," she answered, "that's right. And if you'll come back to my compartment, I'll arrange it right now."

"Oh, but we are approaching Toccoa, and I must get off."

"That's all right; I am quite through, and there'll surely be time." With that, she started back to her compartment, and he followed.

It took her a long time to find her check book in her handbag; it took a longer time to find her fountain pen; and he stood there, not knowing what to say. He just remained silent, not knowing whether she would give him five dollars or five hundred. Finally she got the cap off her pen, opened the check book—and the pen was dry. Knowing that they were already coming into the railroad yards of Toccoa, he hastened to hand her his pen and, lo and behold, it was also out of ink.

Rev. Forrest felt he must have that check, whatever its amount might be, so he said, "Wait a minute, I'll find you a pen." He dashed through the coach and went into the washroom. There he saw a man with several pens showing from his vest pocket. Impetuously he grabbed one of them and started out.

"Come back with my pen!" yelled the man.

"I will in a few minutes, brother," Rev. Forrest called over his shoulder, as he rushed back to the old lady. By now he remembered that all trains stopped at Toccoa to take on water for the locomotives, and that it would be about ten minutes before the train would pull into the station proper.

The lady made out the check and handed it to him. It was for two hundred dollars—twice as much as he needed to meet the loan at the bank. Since he still had a moment or two left, he told her the situation he was in and how he had started home that morning to go to the bank and tell them they would have to wait a little while for their money. But now they wouldn't; it was on time.

Tears came into the eyes of the lady. "Oh, thank the Lord, I have at one time in my life done something when He told me to do it. I'm so happy about this."

While she rejoiced, he took the pen back to its owner and got off the train.

As he walked up the street in Toccoa, he met one of the merchants. He was a kind-hearted man, but was addicted to alcoholism and had been drinking then. Rev. Forrest stopped him on the street, as he always did, and had a word with him. Then he said, "By the way, have you ever seen money that came straight from heaven?"

"No," he replied, "What kind of money do they have up there?"

"Well, I will show you some." He got the check out of his pocket and displayed it.

"Why, that is the same kind of filthy lucre we have down here."

"Oh, no, that is money that came straight from heaven." With that, he told the story of the check.

The merchant was greatly moved, and at about nine o'clock the next morning he was out at Toccoa Falls ringing

119

the front doorbell of the Forrest home. As he wouldn't go into the house, Rev. Forrest sat down on the porch to talk with him—and had the joyous privilege that morning of leading that man to Christ. He died some years after that a sober man; and more than that, he died the death of a Christian. He's alive forevermore.

On this occasion God gave Rev. Forrest twice as much as he was praying for—and a man's soul in addition. Again He proved His Word: *Before they call, I will answer; and while they are yet speaking, I will hear.*

God's resources are unlimited; His methods of supplying needs are manifold. Some time after the instance just mentioned, a similar need arose; and God supplied the money in a quite different, but quite remarkable, way. Again there was a note of one hundred dollars at the bank; it fell due on Saturday—again there seemed to be no way to meet it.

Rev. Forrest was in New York during the week before the note was due, preaching in the Gospel Tabernacle on Eighth Avenue. Between services he kept thinking about that debt and praying that some one in New York would feel led to contribute some money to the school. Nothing had happened, and he was wondering what he'd tell the banker when he returned to Toccoa.

One day he received a note written on beautifully engraved paper. "I wonder who sent me this; I don't know anyone who'd use such fine paper," he thought as he opened the envelope. Naturally, he glanced first at the signature. It was that of Mrs. William Borden, whose family had become very prosperous in the dairy business. "Now what could she want?" he mused as he scanned the note.

Mrs. Borden had written that she was in the service Sunday morning at the Tabernacle. She had received much blessing from Rev. Forrest's message that morning and wanted him to come to see her. He was beside himself.

Imagine—Mrs. Borden sending for him to come to see her! She had set the date for Wednesday evening, so he put on his best "bib and tucker" and went to her house with a great deal of trepidation. He didn't know how to act. Why, even the house she was living in was enough to frighten him—she was renting it from young John Rockefeller.

The colored liveried doorman answered the bell and held out a silver platter for Rev. Forrest's card, and he didn't have one. He simply had to tell the servant who he was.

"Oh, yes," the doorman answered, "Mrs. Borden's looking for you." He took Rev. Forrest into a little reception room and showed him to a certain chair. Mr. Forrest looked upon that chair with some suspicion: it didn't look very substantial. Since he didn't know what else to do, he sat down; and the chair promptly collapsed under him. It was an antique and had been in that steam-heated room so long that all the joints were loose. And just as he went down in a heap in the ruins, Mrs. Borden walked into the room.

"Well!" she said.

The incident did have a humorous angle, and Rev. Forrest laughed. Mrs. Borden then bent double with laughter. "What a way to receive a man!" she exclaimed.

"What a way to come into your home!" he retorted. "Smashing the furniture the first thing!"

That broke the ice—"and nearly broke me, as well," Mr. Forrest later said.

The table was set for Mrs. Borden, her niece, her daughter Joyce, and the guest. There was a maid behind each chair. Rev. Forrest wanted to throw something at the one opposite him, as she watched every mouthful he took. When they sat down, he pulled the napkin from his plate and put it into his lap; and there was something in that napkin! He didn't know what it was, but he felt it drop and grabbed it between his knees. While returning thanks, he was feeling around to see what he could find. The maid, meanwhile, noticed what had happened and was doing her best to keep from laughing. Rev. Forrest went on with the blessing, and for him it surely was a time of thanksgiving—he'd found out what had been in the napkin—a hot roll. He shifted it back up onto his plate before he'd finished praying. Just as he was congratulating himself for handling the situation without the Bordens' noticing, the daughter leaned over and said, "Neat going!"

Nevertheless, they had a lovely visit. Mrs. Borden asked him all about the school. He answered all her questions, but did not mention the note that would fall due in a few days.

After he had returned to the Alliance Home where he was staying while in New York, Rev. Forrest wrote his wife a long letter, telling her about the beautiful Borden home, the fine furnishings, candelabra at each place at the table, the maids and the service, and the events of the evening. He mentioned how nice Mrs. Borden was and what a good time of prayer they'd had together. He concluded with the words: "She never said a word about money."

His gloom vanished the next day. Mrs. Borden sent him a pretty little envelope, with a check in it for one hundred dollars. He had the money to pay the note. After that, as long as she lived, she sent hundreds of dollars to Tococa Falls.

Many times while in the act of prayer, asking God for the supply of some need, Dr. Forrest has caught himself thinking, "Now, who could supply that for us?" Then he has felt rebuked as a still small voice has answered: "You are asking Me for this? It's none of your business through whom it may come. That's My Father's business."

In 1929, the Toccoa Falls Institute was desperately in need of four thousand dollars. Everyone was earnestly praying to God for the supply of this urgent want—really leaving it with Him, asking Him to supply in His own way. In the meantime, arrangements had been made for Rev. Forrest to come to Newark, New Jersey, for an evangelistic campaign to be held in an abandoned theater. Rev. Forrest thought that he could not leave home with that heavy burden resting upon Mrs. Forrest and others; but the call had come, the advertising was out, he was expected to come, and it would not have been fair to cancel the engagement; so he went, believing that God in His own way would supply what seemed to him a huge amount of money. In fact, he couldn't imagine what he could have done about it, had he stayed at home; therefore, he went on, feeling that he was going in the center of His will.

The second night of the meetings two ladies came to Rev. Forrest at the close of the service and told him there was a ninety-two-year-old lady in town who couldn't come to the services because of the bitter cold February weather. She had seen in the papers that he was there, remembered a kindness he had done for her fifteen years before, and was very anxious that he should come to see her.

He explained to the ladies how busy he was both in the day and in the evening and regretted that he couldn't go. They said the old lady would be very much disappointed. He was sorry about that, too, but couldn't see how he could make the visit.

The next night the ladies came back. "You must go see our friend," they insisted. "She says she wants to do something for you to get square with you for the kindness you showed her fifteen years ago."

"I can't imagine who she is or what I did for her," he remonstrated.

"Just the same, you must go see her. She told us that she was going to sit up and wait for you to come tonight after the service; and if you don't come, she'll sit up all night."

"That would be too bad," said the preacher. For this reason he took Mr. Lambert, one of the participating ministers, with him and went to see the old lady. He found her living in a twelve-room house all by herself. She was a widow, with no children and "no kinfolks that care a hoot about me," she said.

When Rev. Forrest arrived, the little old lady explained the "kindness" he'd shown her. It seemed that about fifteen years before, he'd been preaching in a large gospel tent in the Bronx. One night she was a little late for the service and couldn't find a seat near the front. "I was a leetle hard o'hearing and I had to get up front," she told him, "but nobody up there would give me a chair or a seat. Nobody paid any attention to this old lady."

"That was too bad," murmured Rev. Forrest, still wondering how he'd helped.

"Well, finally you saw me standing there, and got up and took your own chair where you'd been sitting on the platform, and brought me that chair. You had to sit on the steps of the platform until time to preach. And I says to myself, says I, 'Now that man's a Christian.' I went to the meetings a good deal after that and I never forgot you; I've prayed for you many times since that. When I saw that you were coming to the city, I thought that this would be the time that I could see you and make you understand how grateful I was for that chair."

They sat around and talked until nearly midnight. Rev. Forrest didn't see her doing anything to get square with him. Finally they had a word of prayer together, and the men got up to leave. As they were going out the front door, Rev. Lambert preceding, their hostess clutched at Rev. Forrest's coat sleeve and whispered, "When could you come back and see me alone?"

"Well," he thought, "I guess I can take a chance on a

124

ninety-two-year-old lady." Aloud he said, "I perhaps could come Sunday afternoon."

"I'll be looking for you."

When he got to her house on Sunday, Rev. Forrest found the old lady very much excited about something. She seemed as happy as a child on Christmas morning; and the first thing she did was to go over to a secretary against the wall and take out a long manila envelope. She handed it to him, cackling and giggling all the while.

He asked, "What's this?"

"Open it and see."

He opened the envelope and found in it nine thousand dollars worth of New Jersey State first mortgage bonds. "Why," he sputtered, "what is this?"

She chortled, "That's for giving me your chair fifteen years ago."

"Well, now," he said, "I'll be giving all the old ladies chairs from now on, but you can't do this."

"Why can't I?" she demanded. "There's plenty more where that came from. I want you to have it."

"Why, you just can't do it."

"Now, wait a minute; that's what they told me in the bank yesterday, when I went to get this stuff."

"Who told you?"

"The secretary to the president of the bank saw me going down to the vault. She followed me down the steps and asked where I was going, and I told her downstairs. She said, 'What are you going to do?' I said, 'Get something out of my box.' 'What?' 'Something.' So she followed me down into the vault, and when I took these things out, she said, 'What are you going to do with that?' I said, 'I'm going to give them away.' 'Why,' she said, 'you can't do that.' I said, 'Who said I can't? This is my stuff, and there's plenty more where this came from; of course I'm going to give it away.' She kept saying, 'It's just not being done.' 'Then it's going to be done *now*.' Well, she argued and argued with me, and then finally went upstairs and brought the president down, and the two of them argued with me from a little after ten to almost eleven o'clock, trying to prove to me that I was an old fool for giving you these securities. Finally I got mad and told them, 'Now, wait a minute, who does this belong to, you or me? I'm ninety-two years old; I'm a widow; I have no children; my kinfolks, the few I have, care little about me now—but you let me die and they'll all come out of the tall grass, all wanting to get their part of it. I'm going to have the fun of doing something with it while I'm living!' So I just put the stuff under my arm and walked out."

Rev. Forrest was deeply moved. Here was more than twice the amount of money that was so desperately needed at this time. He thanked the little lady profusely and then went back to notify Mrs. Forrest that their prayers had been answered.

When he arrived home, Rev. Forrest found that there was more to the story. On the Saturday morning that the little old lady went to the bank in New Jersey, in north Georgia Mrs. Forrest was working out in the yard, putting some bulbs into the ground. She went into the house at about ten o'clock and was in the act of combing her hair and getting ready for the day, when suddenly she was seized with a conviction that she should pray for her husband, that he might contact somebody in the North who would come to their help in this time of distress and supply the four thousand dollars they had to have. The conviction was so pungent that she could not even finish combing her hair until she had called together for a season of prayer the girls who were working around the house. They went before the Lord and were down on their knees from a little after ten until nearly eleven. While that old lady was arguing with the bank president and his secretary, they were approaching the throne of grace, and God heard their prayer and sent the money that was so much needed.

Of this incident, Rev. Forrest later said, "Now had you been in heaven, you would have seen a flash of prayer coming up from the north Georgia hills into heaven and a flash going down to that bank vault in New Jersey, and the old lady picking up that envelope and walking out as she said, 'Who does this belong to, you or me? I'm going to do what I want with it.'"

Chapter Sixteen

*"Say ye to the righteous, that it shall be well with him:
for they shall eat the fruit of their doings."*—Isaiah 3:10

In the lives of His own, God sometimes closes one door
in order to open a far wider field of service. Such has been
the case in the lives of the Forrests. Perhaps, as God tested
Abraham in the offering up of his son Isaac, so He was
testing these young people in the offering of themselves
to the rigors of the mission field. Were they willing to en-
dure the hardships of the missionary, they could be entrusted with the greater task of preparing others to go in
their place.

At any rate, before they were married, Mrs. Forrest felt
that her Lord wanted her in French West Africa as His
representative there. Although engaged to be married and
Rev. Forrest having no leading that way, she with a sincere
desire to please her Lord first, applied to The Christian
and Missionary Alliance to send her to Africa. She was
accepted as a missionary, but rejected for Africa at the time
because of her health. Meanwhile Rev. Forrest seemed
led to Brazil, but the door was closed to him on the eve
of sailing by the death of the man with whom he was to
have gone.

While the Forrests were doing home mission work in
Orlando, they wrote to the Board in New York, asking to be
reconsidered as candidates for the foreign mission field.
They stated in their letter that they would be willing to go
anywhere. The Board wrote back, stating that they were
very happy to read that the Forrests were willing to serve

HADDOCK INN, LAKE VIEW

DORMITORY TENTS

anywhere—and that they were to continue serving right where they were, in Orlando!

With all doors to the foreign field closed to them, the Forrests promised God that they would send others in their stead. By 1935 graduates from Toccoa Falls were actually at work for Christ in Africa, India, China, South America, Central America, Cuba, Costa Rica, the Netherland East Indies, the island of Haiti, and other lands. Today it can truly be said that the sun never sets on the work of graduates of Toccoa Falls Institute.

To see the fruits of one's labors is a soul-thrilling experience. In 1930 the Forrests had this high privilege.

During the nearly twenty years of the school's existence there had been so many difficult places that the Forrests were beginning to be worn out physically. Some of their friends, seeing this, thought that they should get away somewhere. They provided the necessary funds for an extended visit to the mission fields of French West Africa and Palestine, two of the places to which they most desired to go—French West Africa because it was the field to which Mrs. Forrest had felt called thirty years before, and Palestine because it was the land of their Lord.

Through God's providence the load at Toccoa Falls was temporarily lifted, a very fine moving picture camera was given them that fresh views of the field might be brought home, and money was given to buy a Ford automobile for the mission to which they were going. Thus, in many ways, He indicated His pleasure in their going to the field; and they could leave with joyful hearts.

After a farewell meeting in the First Presbyterian Church of Toccoa, the Forrests departed for New York. On February 8 they sailed for France. They spent Mrs. Forrest's birthday in Paris. Then they boarded a ship for Africa.

Their first stop was at Dakar. When Rev. Forrest went to find the American consul, he had his first taste of Africa.

He saw lepers sitting along the roadside. He also noticed men who didn't look like lepers sitting nearby picking off scabs. In answer to his questions, he found that there was an epidemic of small pox in the city and that these natives were picking off small pox scabs.

When they arrived at the American Consulate, he knocked. After a slight scurry inside, a native answered the knock. Ascertaining that the consul was there, Rev. Forrest sent in his card. The servant went back into the dark cavity—all Rev. Forrest could see was the darkness inside, as the sunlight was so bright outside. Then he heard a strange whoop, and somebody came running to the door. It was the consul; he was a Georgia boy who had been to Toccoa many times and who knew the Forrests personally. They in turn were surprised to see him, for they had not known that he was there. Of course, then he was prepared to do anything on earth possible to help them on their trip. They left their trunks with him while they went into the interior, and he put them in touch with the proper people all along the way. In such a way God aided His children in a far land.

They took the same ship and went on down to Conakry, Sierra Leone. Mrs. Forrest had been besieged with illness all the way down the coast. She was so weak that she could scarcely stand. At first the authorities decided that, because of her illness, the Forrests couldn't land at all. "What will they do with us? Surely we haven't come so far only to be doomed to disappointment," they thought anxiously. Meanwhile all the other passengers had gone ashore.

During this period of anxiety one of the missionaries, Harry Watkins from Winston-Salem, North Carolina, had come down to meet the Forrests. When they did not come ashore with the other passengers, he sensed that something was wrong, hired a launch, and started out to the ship. In the confusion he passed the Forrests going to shore, and neither party recognized the other. Finally he came back and met the Forrests at the dock, where they were waiting.

From Conakry the Forrests went by train up to Kankan, the headquarters of The Christian and Missionary Alliance in French West Africa. From that point they covered more than three thousand miles in a Ford automobile, visiting eleven different tribes—four of them cannibal tribes—and sections of the country.

Of great interest was their visiting the remains of a marvelous piece of evangelism accomplished some years before by a native named William Wade Harris. When he was converted, as a boy, in a Methodist mission, he felt called to preach to his own people, but refused to do it. Some years later as he was walking through the bush, he came face to face with a man-eating leopard crouched ready to spring. He cried to God for help, remembered the promise he'd made to God that he'd preach to his own people, and promised the Lord that if He'd deliver him from that leopard, he'd begin at once.

Instantly the leopard wheeled, jumped back through the jungle, and left him. The native kept his word. In a few short years he had established 150 stations. He went from town to town, preaching the good news of salvation. A mighty revival was on among his people. Thousands accepted Christ. The remains of those churches are there yet, many of which are occupied by various mission boards who have gone to that part of the country since then.

The Forrests were accompanied by Mr. Robert Roseberry, superintendent of the Alliance mission in that part of the world, when they went to visit some of these churches. They arrived at the first one just as darkness fell. When the automobile stopped, it was immediately surrounded by a horde of natives. At length the chief of the tribe came down, pushed his way through the crowd and up to the window of the car, and recognized Mr. Roseberry. He turned to a boy standing nearby and said a few words, whereupon the lad wheeled around and ran to a house not very far up the road. In a few seconds he came out of the hut, ringing a bell furiously and crying, "The Man of God has come; the Man of God has come!"

In the dim twilight all wended their way toward what they called a church. It was a thatched grass roof held up with poles and posts. There were no seats; everyone sat cross-legged on the ground. There were a couple of boxes in the front of the room. These had been placed behind a rough board table. Here the visitors sat. Someone placed upon the table a lamp which was nothing but a bowl, with some kind of oil in it and a wick coming out of a spout.

It was a weird scene to see those natives crowd into that place until it was packed, sitting on the floor cross-legged. The guests sat quietly; there was perfect silence; then one native quietly rose to his feet and raised his voice in prayer. He put up his hands, and over the great throng round about came a rough "Ah-meen" all through his prayer. The Forrests couldn't understand what he said, but God evidently understood both the prayer and the reverent "ah-meen's" every now and then.

When the prayer was ended, the congregation began to sing; and there was perfect harmony. Not a one of them had ever seen a note of music, but the harmony was there. They sang an old-time gospel hymn—and how they did sing it! The visitors who sat on the boxes behind that rough board table were so deeply touched that they had to wipe the tears from their eyes.

Later they found that there had not been a missionary to visit that town since Mr. Roseberry had been there many months before. Yet here they were—they worshipped regularly, one day out of seven, sitting in this rough building. With no missionary and no preacher, they repeated over and over again what they had heard. It was a wonderful occasion for the Forrests to remember.

Afterwards, a young lady student from Toccoa Falls Institute was stationed in this same town as a missionary.

When the Forrests arrived at the mission station at Gao, near Timbuktu, they left the Ford automobile there, where it was used for a number of years.

To both Rev. and Mrs. Forrest was given the happy privilege of breaking the bread of life to the missionaries whose stations they visited. They also spoke to native gatherings by means of an interpreter. Thus God, in His tender compassion, allowed them to realize the fulfillment of a dream they had had for thirty years—that of ministering on the foreign field.

After leaving French West Africa, the Forrests visited the Canary Islands, Morocco, Marseilles in France, and Alexandria and Cairo in Egypt. They spent the Easter season in Jerusalem, where Rev. Forrest preached four times on Easter Sunday. Imagine his surprise at being chosen from the many great preachers who were there at that time to preach at the sunrise service before the Garden Tomb of our Lord. This he counts as one of the highest honors bestowed upon him; this experience he will never forget. As he stood in the doorway of the Tomb preaching, a large number of English-speaking people stood in front of him. Behind this congregation were several other groups, each speaking a separate tongue. There were perhaps six or eight different groups, each with their own interpreter standing in front of them. As Rev. Forrest spoke, the interpreters translated his thoughts into their own language, until a babel of sound resulted—but each was hearing the message in his own tongue.

Later in Rome, while visiting some points of interest, the Forrests noticed a group of tourists frequently turning to look at them. Finally a lady came over and said, "Will you please pardon, but is this the Reverend R. A. Forrest who spoke at the Garden Tomb in Jerusalem on Easter Sunday?" When she found it was, she said, "We attended that service and shall never forget the impressions that were made on us at that time." Since then, at least a half dozen times in the States, people have come to Rev. Forrest during evangelistic engagements to tell him that they'd attended that service at the Garden Tomb in Jerusalem.

Rev. and Mrs. Forrest visited England and Scotland, the land of his ancestors, on the way home. While in Scotland he received a cable saying that his father had died in Miami, Florida. Counting the difference in time, he was dying as his son was speaking of the resurrection at the empty tomb.

The Forrests arrived at Toccoa Falls just in time for the graduation exercises on May 29, 1930, bringing back with them a new vision of the mission field, whereby they continued to set fires of missionary zeal blazing in the hearts of the students and others with whom they were to come in contact.

In 1936 Dr. Forrest (for so he was now called) celebrated the twenty-fifth anniversary of the founding of Toccoa Falls Institute by a second trip abroad. This visit around the world had been planned for many months, and in all the plans Mrs. Forrest was to accompany him. However, because of a broken hip and a prolonged illness she was not able to go. She insisted upon her husband's going anyhow, for his own sake and for the sake of the missionaries he would contact and to whom he would be a blessing on the field.

Dr. Forrest left Toccoa early in October for the Pacific Coast, from whence he was to sail for the Far East. He had planned to go west by way of New Orleans, Houston, San Antonio, and El Paso, because he had friends at all these places and had intended to "preach his way" to the coast.

However, a few days before he was to leave Toccoa Falls, he had a letter from his friend, Dr. R. R. Brown, pastor of the Gospel Tabernacle in Omaha, Nebraska, asking him to come that way and speak at a missionary convention he was holding in his tabernacle. He declined. After his refusing a second time by mail, Dr. Brown sent a telegram, urging him to come. Dr. Forrest thought about the invitation much and prayed about it—he might be mistaken, and perhaps he should go by way of Omaha. Finally he decided he would do so and wired Dr. Brown to that effect.

Little did he know why he was led to go to Omaha. He did not know that he was to cross paths at this time with R. G. LeTourneau, a prominent Christian industrialist with a great plant at Peoria, Illinois. Dr. Forrest did not know Mr. LeTourneau and had never heard from him; although Mr. LeTourneau was in the congregation the night that Dr. Forrest spoke, they did not meet each other.

At the close of the service, Mr. LeTourneau hunted out Dr. Brown and asked him, "Who is this guy? Where does he live? What does he do? Where is he going?"

Dr. Brown told him about the Toccoa Falls Institute. He also mentioned that Dr. Forrest was starting a trip around the world to visit former students on the mission field.

Mr. LeTourneau went back to Peoria; Dr. Forrest went on west. Still they had not met. Two or three nights later, Mr. LeTourneau called Toccoa Falls to learn how he could reach Dr. Forrest before he sailed. His secretary answered that he was preaching that night in Hollywood, California. Mr. LeTourneau called Hollywood, only to find that Dr. Forrest had left three or four hours previously for Seattle on the way to Japan. Fortunately, Dr. Forrest had left a forwarding address, and this was given to Mr. LeTourneau.

Dr. Forrest was to sail at ten o'clock on a Saturday morning. The night before, he called at the apartment of two former students (whose address he had given as his forwarding address) to pick up any last communications from home. After visiting a short time, he started to say good-by, as it was now ten p.m. He heard footsteps and turned to see a messenger boy coming up the steps with a letter in his hand, a letter marked "Special Delivery Air Mail." He had an intuition that the letter belonged to him. In answer to his question, the boy replied, "Why, yes, that's the name, Forrest."

Dr. Forrest took the letter and went back into the apartment to read it. It was from the industrialist, R. G. LeTourneau, who told him what Dr. Brown had said in the church that night and how it had given him an idea. He thought it would be nice if Dr. Forrest had some money in his pocket as he went round the world to give to folks in a "tough spot." He was enclosing a check for one thousand dollars. Dr. Forrest was to use his own judgment as to what to do with it—just report when he got back as to how it had been used.

One can imagine how thrilled Dr. Forrest was at this idea. He decided to convert that check into $10 and $20 traveler's checks. Since his ship was to leave at ten in the morning, he was at the door of the bank when it opened at nine. He had a few anxious minutes, for the bank did not know him or the check either. Remembering that it was made upon a Stockton, California, bank (a town where Mr. LeTourneau had formerly lived), Dr. Forrest told the cashier: "You call the bank; I'll pay the line charge."

While the call was being made, he dashed out to attend to some last minute errands. Upon his return to the bank, the vice-president met him at the door, saying, "Brother, how many more checks like that would you like to have us cash? There's ten million dollars behind that one." Dr. Forrest went to the mission field with all his pockets full of ten dollar checks.

He dodged into a five-and-ten-cent store next door to

the bank and bought a handful of five-cent receipt books. Everywhere he went he had a receipt book and a ten dollar check in his pocket. He made everybody sign the receipt in his own language. Since he had the advantage of the exchange in the interior of China, Borneo, and some other countries, he brought home $1,086.00 worth of receipts!

Coming across the Atlantic he numbered those receipts and wrote a little paragraph on the back of each one, stating to whom he'd given money, why he'd given it, and what had been done with it. The results of those checks were wonderful. For instance, in Korea there was a native girl who had become a Christian only a few weeks before. Her father told her he was going to have to sell her as a concubine to an old man. He was to get forty dollars for her. When Dr. Forrest heard of this, he bought himself a girl. He paid the money, and then sent the girl to a Christian school. Things like that happened in many places all around the world.

The receipts were mailed to Mr. LeTourneau as soon as Dr. Forrest landed in New York. In a few days there came an answer, stating how happy the industrialist was over the way the money had been handled. "Come see me," the letter concluded.

It was several months before Dr. Forrest could arrange a visit with Mr. LeTourneau. The outcome of the whole affair was that Mr. LeTourneau figured that if Dr. Forrest could be trusted with $1,000.00 on the other side of the world, he might be trusted with $10,000.00 on this side. Mr. LeTourneau sent a check for this amount to the Toccoa Falls Institute.

(Later the paths of these two men were to continue to cross, as Mr. LeTourneau was to establish a plant near Toccoa, Georgia.)

Dr. Forrest's second trip abroad was far more extensive than the first; he was gone for five months and covered

25,000 miles in his tour around the world. It was his purpose to visit the mission fields of the former students of Toccoa Falls who were now serving on the foreign fields; this he did, and contacted many other stations, both Presbyterian and Alliance, besides.

God is tender to His children. Although He did not permit the Forrests to go as missionaries to the foreign field, surely He walked with them as they were given the opportunity of seeing themselves multiplied in the Toccoa Falls graduates who had been sent forth "into His harvest." *His compassions fail not—great is (His) faithfulness.*

Chapter Seventeen

"A woman that feareth the Lord, she shall be praised. Give her of the fruit of her hands; and let her own works praise her in the gates."—PROVERBS 31:30b, 31

THE STORY OF Dr. Forrest and the Toccoa Falls Institute would be incomplete without special reference to Mrs. Forrest; indeed, the story of the school would have been impossible without her presence, help, and guidance. From the earliest days it has been her task to "tarry by the stuff" as her husband has been active all over the world in evangelistic work and in making both the needs and the work of his school known. She, too, will receive her reward. God has promised: *But as his part is that goeth down to the battle, so shall his part be that tarrieth by the stuff: they shall part alike.*

As a child Evelyn Drennen was deprived of many pleasures which children enjoy because she was frail and delicate. Through a fall at the age of three her right arm was broken and left clavicle knocked out of place. A good physician set the broken arm, which was soon well; but the depressed joint of the clavicle bone was not discovered for many years. The constant pressure on the bronchial nerve, meanwhile, caused spasmodic asthma from which she suffered intensely at times. Nevertheless, she attended the State Normal College at Newark, Delaware, and The Missionary Training Institute at Nyack, New York, where she was an exceptionally fine student. She was very active in extra-curricular work, as well. She then became a full-time Christian worker for The Christian and Missionary

Alliance in Oil City, Pennsylvania. The Lord honored her complete surrender to Him and desire to serve Him by healing her of these dread attacks of asthma.

After her marriage, Mrs. Forrest worked side by side with her husband, in whatever capacity seemed necessary. Having had before her, during her girlhood, the example of a godly mother who taught her daughter not only to live well but to be a true servant of Jesus Christ, Mrs. Forrest's consecrated life fitted her well for the place she was to fill— both as helpmeet for one of God's chosen servants, and as Bible teacher in her own right.

Mrs. Forrest has always been an indefatigable laborer for the Lord. She greatly enlarged the work at Oil City during her term of service there; she transferred her enthusiastic efforts to the flatlands around Orlando, leaving indelible results there when she moved to Atlanta to help encourage the small group of Alliance folks at 79 Capitol Avenue; and she became a "tower of strength" during the establishment and first twenty-five years of growth at Toccoa Falls. Thousands recall with thanksgiving her ministry as a Bible teacher both at the Institute and in classes conducted within a hundred and fifty mile radius of Toccoa Falls.

When the Forrests moved to Toccoa Falls, Mrs. Forrest's responsibilities greatly increased. She it was who supervised the arranging of the rooms, the planning of the meals for both students and guests, the cleaning and laundering, and the other tasks involved in running a fifty-room hotel and school combined. She was the one who scoured the countryside for food and who listened to complaints when it didn't suit the guests. "Now we have menu cards and all the guests feel much better pleased," she wrote after one such incident. At another time when the responsibility for such a large task overwhelmed her, she wrote, "May the dear Lord direct for we are not equal to the situation." Results surely indicate that He did.

Mrs. Forrest was a "born teacher." Whether directing a girl as to how to make beds or standing before a class expounding the Word of God, she did so with rare artistry. She *wanted* the young people under her influence to learn.

A few years after the inception of the Toccoa Falls Institute a small group of women appealed to Mrs. Forrest to start a Women's Bible Class at Toccoa, Georgia. She responded to the appeal and for many years gave them a consistent Bible study course. In 1923, at the request of a group of high school girls in Toccoa, she formed a class for their benefit. These girls met after school hours once a week. Each class meeting saw an increase in attendance over the preceding week.

For a number of years Mrs. Forrest accompanied her husband to many conventions, teaching women's and children's classes. She also sponsored groups of young people from the Institute on their trips to various cities throughout the South. As the young folks would play, sing, and speak to church groups, Mrs. Forrest, too, would minister by teaching from the Holy Word. However, she was destined to have a large independent ministry through her outstanding Bible teaching.

Her first class outside of Toccoa, and incidentally her largest, was taught on Friday evening of each week at the Gospel Tabernacle in Atlanta. With an opening attendance of more than two hundred persons, the class was conducted weekly for four years, attendance growing to 750 members, persons eager to know more about the Word of God. Seventy-three members of the class had a perfect attendance and study record for the four years and were awarded certificates. An article by Charles DuBose in "Southern Greetings," November, 1923, says of this class:

> "What an inspiring sight it is to see the upraised Bibles, hundreds of them, at a given signal, and to see the eager interest shining in the faces of the class.
>
> "The method of study is intensely interesting. Mrs.

141

Forrest presents the broad outlines which stand out like mountain peaks on the mental vision and can therefore be easily remembered. This is called Bible Synthesis, and because of the lack of minor details there is not a dry moment as the lesson progresses. . . . At the end of each lesson Mr. Forrest supplements all that has been said with a helpful and spicy summary, calling especial attention to the spiritual lessons conveyed through the text of the evening.

"Who can measure the abundance of grace and blessing that have entered hundreds of lives because of this ministry of the Word?"

At the urgent request of Dr. J. Sproles Lyon, who was then pastor of the First Presbyterian Church of Atlanta, Mrs. Forrest taught a Bible Class in that church for two years. She acceded to further requests and taught similar classes in Asheville, North Carolina; Greenville, Spartanburg, and Anderson, South Carolina; and over WTFI in Toccoa, Georgia.

Such an extensive field of labor, in addition to her tasks as Matron of Girls and Bible teacher at Toccoa Falls, entailed a great deal of self-sacrifice—and even physical discomfort.

Consider, for example, only one of the weekly trips to Asheville, 135 miles away. Roads were then unpaved. On this particular occasion, because of heavy rains the Forrests left Toccoa for Asheville immediately after the Sunday morning service at which Rev. Forrest preached—they wanted to be sure that they would get to Asheville in time for the *Monday evening* Bible Class! They left the church without stopping to eat. After driving several miles through the mud, they got stuck. Rev. Forrest got out in the rain and pushed the heavy old Buick as Mrs. Forrest manipulated the gears. As the car edged forward, he climbed back in, soaking wet. At Tallulah Falls, about twenty-five miles from home, the Buick bogged down again. No amount of pushing could extricate it; at last they had to give up and wait until someone came along to give them aid. They huddled together in the car—uncomfortable, tired, cold, and hungry. Mr. Forrest was soaked to the skin; his wife touchingly tried to warm him by cuddling up as close as she could. All afternoon and night they waited; at eight the next morning one lone man found them and got four mules to pull them out of the mire.

They continued their trip, arriving at Asheville late in the afternoon. Their lodging was furnished them week by week; this time provision had been made for them to stay at Kenilworth Inn, the most exclusive hotel at that time in the city. The Forrests looked almost like tramps by this time; their clothes were so wet and wrinkled that they couldn't even enter the front door, but were taken through the servants' entrance and up their stairway to the room. They didn't have extra clothes; they had to send theirs out to be pressed dry while they waited.

It was nearly six o'clock before they looked presentable. They were nearly famished, not having eaten since Sunday morning. As they came down the steps and walked through the lobby, they had to pass the dining room. They looked in and saw the crisp linen tablecloths and sparkling silver; they smelled the delicious odors of food—but didn't have money enough to eat in a place like that, so they got into their muddy car and drove downtown to a clean cheap restaurant for supper. After this they went on to the Tabernacle where Mrs. Forrest uncomplainingly taught her class. No one knew the vicissitudes of that trip.

The next morning as they were planning to go downtown for breakfast, the telephone rang. When Rev. Forrest answered, the manager of the hotel was on the line. "Will you soon be down to breakfast?" he queried.

Rev. Forrest stammered, "Why, we thought we'd go downtown."

"What's the matter? Doesn't our cook suit you? You

know, you're our guests, and we'd like to have you eat with us."

Rev. Forrest thanked him and hung up. Dazed, he told Mrs. Forrest how they'd passed up a marvelous meal the night before and how he must go down and apologize for his behavior.

She smiled sweetly and replied, "A lot of Christians are just like us. Just as we failed to take advantage of a bountiful meal last evening, they fail to feed upon the blessed Word of God, the Bread of Life. When it's too late, we realize how much we've missed. But come, let's be dilatory no longer. We shall have breakfast at Kenilworth Inn—and we can order anything on the menu. Praise the Lord!"

Mrs. Forrest's personal life has, of necessity, been one of self-denial. Her entire married life has been characterized by continuous separations from her husband as he has been called to evangelistic efforts throughout the country. Many a month has passed during which she has seen him for only one or two days between engagements. Yet she has labored diligently at home, praising God for the opportunities that both were given to serve Him.

Such a full and varied teaching ministry left Mrs. Forrest practically no time for a personal life. For example, at one time she purchased a pattern for a beautiful butterfly afghan, hoping that someday she'd find time to crochet it. After keeping the pattern for several years, one December day she sadly—almost tearfully—consigned it to the waste basket, acknowledging the fact that she was too busy to make something she didn't have to have. The Lord is gracious; He honored both her labors and her desire: on Christmas morning of that year Mrs. Forrest opened a box from one of her sisters—it contained a butterfly afghan exactly like her pattern! Then the tears really did flow as she marveled anew at the goodness of God in providing exactly that for which she had been yearning.

In Mrs. Forrest's life there have been many testings, for

Satan does not willingly loosen his grip on either the bodies or souls of those who have been redeemed by the blood of Jesus. One of the most severe of these testings began during the Christmas holidays, 1923. Mrs. Forrest had not been feeling well; at Christmas time she contracted a heavy cold, which settled in the right side of her abdomen, causing high fever and inflammation. The swelling grew to an enormous size and was intensely painful, so much so that she could not even allow the bedcovers to touch it at night.

It was with great difficulty that she kept up her regular classes at the Institute and in various cities. Strangely enough, although she stood before her classes in great physical weakness, she was free from pain during the actual teaching.

At first she did not want to go to a doctor, hoping that she would soon be better, but the swelling grew so bad that it caused great concern to all who were aware of it.

On February 8, 1924, Rev. Forrest met Dr. Jeff Davis, then the outstanding physician of northeast Georgia, in Toccoa and impulsively told him of his wife's condition. After calling on her, Dr. Davis became much concerned and urged Rev. Forrest to take Mrs. Forrest to Atlanta to see Dr. Elizabeth Broach, the finest diagnostician for women in the South. "It may be malignant," he added.

Rev. Forrest answered, "Why, Dr. Jeff, we're going to Atlanta tomorrow for Mrs. Forrest's Bible Class anyhow. We'll go see Dr. Broach. She's a very fine Christian and a long-time friend of ours."

Dr. Jeff said, "She can't take a Bible class in this condition."

"We'll go to Atlanta anyhow."

They went directly from the railroad station by taxi to Dr. Broach's office. After examining Mrs. Forrest thoroughly, Dr. Broach spoke privately to Rev. Forrest. With tears in her eyes she gave her report: "Rev. Forrest, I'm seriously afraid there's something terribly wrong with Mrs.

Forrest, and I fear it's malignant. However, I don't want you to take my word for it, but insist you go to see an X-ray man."

She phoned and made an immediate appointment. The Forrests took a taxi to his office and had the X-ray made. When the technician came out of the darkroom with the negative, it showed very plainly what he called "the mass." He, too, was very much disturbed as he told them that there was a malignant growth larger than his doubled fist and that it had involved three of the vital organs.

The Forrests spent the rest of the day in their hotel room in quiet meditation and prayer. They had lost all appetite for food. They placed Mrs. Forrest wholly on the altar, ready for either sacrifice or service. As the hour for the Bible Class drew near, the Holy Spirit made it plain to Mrs. Forrest that God would give her strength to get up, dress, and go teach her class. Her husband made her promise to speak only thirty minutes and then slip out quietly while he closed and explained to the class her reason for leaving early.

While sitting on the platform during the opening songs and prayer, Mrs. Forrest was so nauseated that she could hardly sit still, but as she stepped before that class of more than five hundred people, she looked up with her whole heart and soul lifted in prayer and whispered, "Jesus, I take Your life for this service." And God answered. At first great beads of perspiration trickled out of her hair and rolled down the back of her neck; but as she went on, the pain lessened. At the end of thirty minutes she stopped and stepped to a side door, where Mr. Tom Latham, owner of a jewelry store, waited to take her back to the hotel.

After she was gone, Rev. Forrest stepped to the front of the platform and told the class just what was the matter with her. Then he witnessed a most impressive sight: those several hundred people just involuntarily went down like grain going down before a wind; as they bowed their heads, there went up an involuntary groan, seemingly from everyone in the crowd. He thought to himself: "If I were God, I couldn't turn that down."

After a season of prayer in behalf of Mrs. Forrest, the meeting was concluded, and Rev. Forrest hurried back to the hotel room. There he found his wife on her knees by the side of the bed, laughing and crying and crying and laughing and doing both at the same time. He was petrified; he didn't know whether she was dying or what was the trouble.

Catching sight of her husband, Mrs. Forrest cried happily, "Sweetheart, I've been healed!"

"You've been what?" He was stunned.

"I've been healed. See, that thing's gone and there's no pain at all!"

They spent the rest of that night praising the Lord. The next morning Rev. Forrest said, "Now, listen, I've seen so many people who said they were sick and they were not. We have the word of three physicians that there was something seriously wrong with you. Then I have seen other folks who thought they were healed, and they were not. Let's go back over the same ground we covered yesterday; let's have another X-ray made this morning, go see Dr. Broach again, and then go home and tell Dr. Davis what has happened."

Without telling the X-ray technician why, the Forrests insisted that he take another picture. It was actually comical to see his expression as he came out of the darkroom with that second negative. He said, "There's something radically wrong with this; it's not the same as it was yesterday."

"No," responded the Forrests, "there's nothing wrong with it—it's *right!*"

With tears in his eyes the technician stated, "Now, that's a miracle."

They next went to Dr. Broach's office. Dr. Broach took

Mrs. Forrest again into her private office and examined her. In a few minutes she came out beside herself. She was crying and laughing and praising the Lord. She said, "I've seen what I've been wanting to see ever since I've been in professional life. I've been waiting for it. I have now seen it—a one-hundred per cent supernatural miracle. I'll stake my reputation as a diagnostician on the fact that that thing was there yesterday. I know it's gone today. How could that happen except God did it supernaturally?"

The Forrests still have the two X-ray negatives. Thereafter, when Satan would tempt them sorely, they'd get out the two pictures and show them to him—one with the trouble and the second with the trouble gone.

With Rev. Forrest's acceptance, in 1926, of the pastorate of the First Presbyterian Church of Toccoa, Mrs. Forrest became active in the women's work there, teaching the Women's Bible Class in Sunday school for several years. She served as Secretary of Spiritual Life in the Women's Auxiliary for seven years; on the Presbyterial level she was Chairman of Group III for two years and was elected and installed as president in 1936. Illness limited her service there to an advisory capacity.

In addition to her trip abroad previously mentioned, Mrs. Forrest has also been privileged to visit former students who are now in active Christian service in Cuba, particularly those engaged in Presbyterian work.

On August 25, 1935, great personal tragedy struck the Forrests—tragedy which has affected untold others besides. The day started ordinarily enough. It was Sunday morning; the Forrests were leaving the house to go to the Presbyterian Church in Toccoa; Mrs. Forrest discovered that she didn't have a handkerchief and hurried back into the bedroom for one. In her haste she slipped on a throw rug on the polished floor and fell. She felt and heard a snap; when she tried to get up, she realized that something drastic had happened.

Examination proved that she had broken her left hip. She spent eighteen weeks in a plaster cast; since the bone seemed to be properly healed, she began to use two canes to move around. Then the hip began to trouble her; upon investigation it was found that the bone had not healed at all but, on the contrary, was beginning to shrink. The ends of the bone were refreshed and a silver pin inserted. Some time later the hip was still causing tremendous pain, so another examination was made. At this time it was discovered that nearly three inches of the bone next to the hip socket had decayed away and was no more. Since that time, Mrs. Forrest has been very close to the Borderland time and time again. She has been under the care of the best specialists in America and has made remarkable recovery from recurring attacks of illness brought on as a result of the broken hip. Several times small slivers of bone from the hip have caused huge ulcers; the slivers have been removed and the ulcers lanced and drained.

Through the intense suffering of these attacks, which have occurred periodically since her fall, Mrs. Forrest has uttered not one cry or groan. Students who have worked in the Forrest cottage have walked softly past her bedroom door, never to hear an outcry, but only a soft "Praise the Lord" every now and then.

For ten years after her fall, Mrs. Forrest continued to teach her Bible classes whenever she was able; since that time she has been unable to meet classes. This is indeed a testing for her, as she has always loved to teach, especially to teach the Word of God.

It seems strange that God saw fit, at one time, to heal Mrs. Forrest miraculously but did not do so again. Those who have been near to the Forrests and their school have been unable to understand why Mrs. Forrest should be laid aside. Through the years she has been a strong factor and spiritual force which has greatly affected the character of the school and the lives of the students. Her teaching

149

has always given spiritual impetus in addition to intellectual instruction. Her character and daily life have been so consistent with her Bible teaching that her influence upon the students is one of the sweetest memories they have carried from the school. All those who have been her students or fellow-workers remember Mrs. Forrest's consecrated, self-sacrificing labors and her earnest prayer life.

Only the Master understands why she should be placed in the role of spectator rather than participant during the last few years. Suffice it to say, He knows best. *For now we see through a glass, darkly; but then face to face: now I know in part; but then shall I know even as also I am known.*

Mrs. Forrest has been a consecrated servant of the Lord throughout these many years; her valiant spirit and assistance have made possible the Toccoa Falls Institute of today; her students "arise up, and call her blessed"; her influence, though passive, still permeates the campus; her love and affection spur on her husband as he continues to labor.

Chapter Eighteen

"As thou goest, step by step, I will open up the way before thee."—PROVERBS 4:12, HEBREW TRANSLATION

THE 1930's were years of anxiety for much of the world—at Toccoa Falls there were moments of concern, too; but these were mingled with times of rejoicing, as the Lord provided for His own.

To be sure, the Institute was affected by the years of depression and drouth. There was the time, early in the thirties, when Rev. Forrest sold his new Buick in order to buy food for the students—since that time he has been amply repaid for his sacrifice, not only in seeing those young people in full-time service, but in a material way, as well: former students and friends have, on more than one occasion, given him a new automobile when the need arose.

There were the weeks when the students and staff members drank sassafras tea—because there was no money to buy the regular kind and Will Prather, the colored cook, took a shovel and dug sassafras roots. The tea tasted good, just the same; and the philosophy which Will, a fine humble Christian, gave was better. At the special dinner before the Christmas holidays one year, the students asked Will to make a speech. He came into the dining room, took off his cook's hat, and said, "Well now, all I have to say to you-all is, if you find yourself off on the wrong road, don't get excited. Just turn around and come on back." Dr. Forrest remarks that many sermons an hour long haven't said any more than that.

Those were the days when the students (about a hundred of them) drank lots of milk, ate lots of vegetables that they'd helped grow, consumed a great deal of fruit, and filled all the empty spots with bread and preserves. Former students look back to those days with joy. Everybody knew everyone else and the fellowship was wonderful. Rev. Forrest, true to his nature, never wanted to turn anyone down who wished to do the Lord's work. Some students came for only ten dollars a month. Some didn't pay anything, but worked extra time to pay for their board and tuition.

In a sense, however, the depression affected the Toccoa Falls Institute for good. Because of it a C. C. C. Camp was started in north Georgia; it was located on property leased from the school, the flat just to the south of the main campus. The C. C. C. boys built roads, paths, firebreaks, and things like that all through the nearby woods. They laid a walk of native stone from Gate Cottage to Falls Park. In these and other ways they improved the appearance of the campus. The school also benefited insofar as food was concerned, for when too much was prepared for the C. C. C. boys, the cooks sent the balance to the Falls kitchen.

When this camp was disbanded, the Government turned over to the Institute lumber representing more than four thousand dollars in value, including their barracks. The barracks were very rough, with the roughest kind of floor and battens up and down on the outside of the building. In 1934 this building was renovated; new flooring was laid, the building was cut up into rooms with permanent partitions erected, and the outside was weatherboarded. This structure, called Ralls Dormitory, has been used as living quarters for thirty-five to forty young men each year and has been a blessing throughout the years.

A highlight of the thirties was the bestowal upon Mr. Forrest of the title "Doctor." On May 27, 1936, the Toccoa Falls Institute felt highly honored as its president and

152

founder was granted the degree of Doctor of Divinity by Bob Jones University. Although reticent about accepting this honor, Dr. Forrest surely deserved it.

During the first twenty-five years of the Institute's existence, educational standards in schools all over the United States advanced greatly. Dr. Forrest saw to it that the Toccoa Falls Institute kept step: in 1937 a four-year Bible College was initiated, consisting of two years of Bible training and two years of liberal arts. Approval of this step was given by the State of Georgia in 1939; at that time the Georgia State Legislature granted authority to the Bible College to grant the degree of Bachelor of Arts in Biblical Education. In keeping with the original purpose of the school, that of offering intensive Bible training to those who have not had the privilege of finishing high school, the Institute has continued to grant two and three-year certificates.

In the fall of 1938 the National Youth Administration, another governmental project launched because of the continued depression, began its Residential Project at Toccoa Falls. Before many months had passed, the Institute was filled to and beyond capacity with students. There were more than four hundred in attendance, most of them from twenty-one counties in Georgia. A fine Christian man was in charge of the Georgia division of the N. Y. A. While students were required to take vocational work, he also approved of their taking high school and Bible College subjects, as well.

Since the school didn't have to take everybody, the group attending was a fine, carefully-picked set, containing some of the best students ever to attend the Institute. Toccoa Falls graduates were sought after by the business and industrial world to fit many important positions.

Courses were offered in crafts, home economics, shop, agriculture, and radio. Four buildings of native stone were constructed by the N. Y. A. group for use in instruction in these fields. These were the Shop Building, which has since been destroyed by fire; the Agricultural Building, which is now being used to house the shop department and the freezer locker; the Radio Building, which has been converted into Ring Music Hall; and the Home Economics Building, a lovely two-story building near the Falls known as Gate Cottage and now used as living quarters for staff members and some married students.

Young men who graduated from the shop course had no difficulty in procuring jobs as machinists. Many went to work in the LeTourneau plant nearby.

An excellent commercial department turned out dozens of graduates each year. In one year alone twenty-one girls and one fellow went to Washington, D. C., where they were hired immediately by the Government. Some of them are in Washington yet.

As he passed through Washington one time, Dr. Forrest stopped to see one of these girls, who was working for a hardboiled Marine officer. While waiting for her, he engaged the officer in conversation, asking, "How is she getting along?"

"Huh—huh—" the officer cleared his throat in a grandiose kind of way. "Let me tell you something, Doc, that girl is tops. She's tops! She knows her job. You did a wonderful job training her. She knows exactly what to do and how to do it." Again he drawled, "She's tops!" Then he went on: "And there's something else about her, Doc. Lemme tell you something. I'm not a very religious man but, Doc, that girl is a Christian. She's the kind I've always heard about, and the kind I'd like to be. That girl's a real Christian and I'm sold on her."

Similar testimonies were given wherever Toccoa Falls graduates were employed. Those students supported by the N. Y. A. carried the Institute through the depression.

At the same time they created a very definite need for enlarged building facilities.

Because of the influx of students under the N. Y. A., housing had become an acute problem. Likewise, the student body had outgrown dining room and kitchen accommodations. The chapel was filled to overflowing. Gymnasium facilities were entirely inadequate, the only space for indoor activities being the lobby of Ralls Dormitory.

To provide for the resulting needs, Dr. Forrest, along with the Executive Committee, determined upon an ambitious project—the erection of a four-story structure. This large building would be the pride of the campus and of northeast Georgia as well. At the time the decision to build was made, there were no funds on hand for building, with perhaps the exception of one or two hundred dollars.

Characteristically, Dr. Forrest asked the students and staff members to miss one meal and to fast and pray for money. Most of them did so. The next morning the boys went out and began to clear and break ground for the building. The old laundry was torn down, stumps were plowed up, and excavation for the basement was begun. Step by step the Lord supplied the need. Approximately half the money for the building was given by one man— the man who had entrusted Dr. Forrest with the thousand dollars at the time of his trip around the world.

After Mr. LeTourneau (for it was he) became interested in Toccoa Falls, he came down to visit. He liked the school, the country, and the people; and suggested that he'd like to build a plant somewhere in the South, perhaps at Toccoa. Although nothing further was said at that time, sometime later he sent Dr. Forrest $10,000.00 to buy him some land on which to build a plant at Toccoa. He wanted a thousand acres or more on the railroad and near Toccoa Falls.

The original purchase was eleven hundred acres. On that property Mr. LeTourneau built a plant that brought millions of dollars into circulation in Toccoa and Stephens County and increased the freight receipts for the Southern Railway over a thousand per cent. Because of Mr. LeTourneau's being a Christian, great spiritual blessing has resulted from the conferences and other meetings of this sort brought to his conference grounds near Toccoa.

Mr. LeTourneau spent considerable time at Toccoa Falls while his plant was under construction. He noted with interest the progress being made on the new building being erected there, and from time to time handed Dr. Forrest a check for a thousand or two thousand dollars to be used in purchasing materials or labor. Mr. LeTourneau gave altogether about half the money needed for the beautiful brick building; in gratitude to him for his generous gifts the structure was called LeTourneau Hall. It housed the gymnasium—which was also used as an auditorium, a lovely dining room seating six hundred, and dormitory space for fifty girls. Mr. LeTourneau also built five steel dormitories, each containing twelve rooms and used largely as living quarters for boys and young men.

A co-op plan was set up, whereby a limited number of men students could support themselves in school by working at the LeTourneau plant. Thus the layman and the schoolman worked together to help youths get a Christian education.

So it was that, during the latter part of the 1930's, the Toccoa Falls Institute made phenomenal growth. From a small school, handling approximately seventy-five students at a time, by 1940 it had grown to a school of four hundred —with representatives that year from twenty-six states, sixty-six Georgia counties, Canada, Cuba, and China. This exceptional development, moreover, was kept steady and sound because of the solid foundations previously laid.

Thanks be unto God! During the ten years when most of the world was retrenching, He had continued to smile on His children down in northeast Georgia—He had permitted them to see soldiers for Christ in action all round the world, and He had not only preserved, but tremendously expanded, the facilities of the school which they had founded, the Toccoa Falls Institute.

Chapter Nineteen

"Now unto him that is able to do exceeding abundantly above all that we ask or think, according to the power that worketh in us, . . . be glory."—EPHESIANS 3:20, 21a

LIKE THE RECURRENT THEME of a great symphony is the reiteration of praise to God for miracles wrought in the hills of northeast Georgia. Truly is He able to do "exceeding abundantly above" the wildest imagination of man. God waits to pour out His blessing upon any movement sponsored by a man who *believes* His promises and *appropriates* them.

In conversation with His disciples Jesus said: *Therefore I say unto you, What things soever ye desire, when ye pray, believe that ye receive them, and ye shall have them.*

Dr. Forrest believes that Christ still means these words, and he has gone forward in faith, confident that the miracles will be wrought. Sufficient evidence to bear out this fact can be found in the early years of the 1940's.

In the October, 1940, issue of the "Toccoa Falls News," a quarterly published by the Institute, Dr. Forrest listed several problems confronting the school.

"The abnormal expansion of the past three years from one hundred to more than four hundred students has made it necessary for much additional equipment, and here are some opportunities for somebody.

"First, increased class room space is absolutely imperative. Classes are now being held in every conceivable corner and the inconvenience reduces efficiency. We have begun excavation for a classroom building which will provide eight classrooms and a school commissary. Why not build it as a memorial?

"We are building up a fine herd of registered Guernsey cattle to provide milk for our students who are now consuming daily around eighty gallons of milk. The State Board of Health has told us on their last inspection that our barn is inadequate for so many cows, and it is imperative that we build a new barn. This would cost three thousand dollars.

"It is impossible to seat all our students at the same time in our chapel for religious services. What a beautiful memorial a church building on the campus to be used for no other purpose but public worship would be!

"We now have four and even five students crowded into a room where ordinarily there would be two. The management has been put to its wits' end to know how to take care of all the students who want to come."

Knowing that God is both willing and able, Dr. Forrest, along with the Institute family and friends, sought Him in prayer, asking for the money necessary to relieve the strain. And to what end? To the end that—within the next five years—all but one of these proposed projects became a fact!

A short time after the article quoted above appeared in the "News," Dr. Forrest received a single dollar from a friend, who designated it especially for the new barn needed. He thanked both the friend and God for the dollar, which he felt was an "earnest" of the building funds to come. Within six months enough money had been received to enable the buying and sawing of all the lumber. By December of the same year, two modern dairy barns were completely built, paid for, and in use. The smaller one is a strictly modern milking barn, with every up-to-date dairy facility. The larger building is known as the sleeping barn, where the cows have adequate protection against rain and cold. These barns stand along the roadside near the entrance to Toccoa Falls.

During the years which have followed, the dairy supervisors have kept pace with all necessary improvements, until today the herd is considered one of the best in northeast Georgia, providing nearly enough returns from milk that is sold to pay for the milk that the students use.

The old barn, one of the oldest buildings on the campus, was built in 1913. After it was condemned and the new barns built, the question arose as to what to do with it. Finally, in view of lack of space for incoming students and after carefully considering the situation, the authorities decided to renovate the old barn completely and to turn it into a dormitory for college men. "The building was condemned for cows, so we put boys in it," Dr. Forrest banters. Actually, when the barn was remodeled, the only original parts left were the outer walls and the roof. An up-to-date steam laundry occupied one wing of the first floor; an apartment for workers was constructed in the other wing; upstairs, which originally was the hay loft, there were accommodations for twenty-four boys, plus an apartment for the laundry supervisor. This building, still in use, was named Morrison Hall. It looks very little like the original barn, and constitutes a beauty spot instead of an eyesore on the campus. Thus the Lord answered the need for extra living space.

The third imperative necessity mentioned in the "News" was a classroom building. Although there were twenty-two teachers, there were only nine classrooms available. Four hundred students were trying to crowd into the classrooms that had been built for one hundred—and they didn't seem to fit! With such an acute need, Dr. Forrest decided to start digging a hole for the foundation of the building, and then trust God to send the money to continue putting up the walls of the structure.

For some time there was only the gaping hole that the students had dug. Finally enough money came in for the foundations for the building. While those were being laid,

1. David Ovens Student Center
2. LeTourneau Hall
3. Earl Hall
4. Morrison Hall
5. Toccoa Falls, 186 feet high
6. Chapel and Library
7. Stewart Dormitory
8. The Challenge—Student Body
9. Administration Building

Dr. Forrest received a letter from a Mr. John A. Earl, telling how much blessing he had received by listening to Dr. Forrest's radio program on Sunday morning and asking Dr. Forrest to "please come see me."

Since the Second World War was now in progress and gasoline was rationed, Dr. Forrest had to delay his visit several weeks until he was in the neighborhood to conduct a funeral service. From the church he set out to call on Mr. Earl, who lived so far back in the woods that a local boy had to point out the way. The drive was beautiful, as the road paralleled the creek and was overhung by huge trees. At length they arrived at a very comfortable cottage, albeit without many of the modern conveniences such as electricity and running water.

Mr. and Mrs. Earl lived there alone. Mr. Earl told Dr. Forrest that he had two reasons in wanting him to call: first, he wanted to tell him how much God had done for him, and second, he had a business proposition to present. He said, "I have some property on which I owe some money. As I'm getting along in years, I want you to take that property and, in return, give my wife and me some kind of security for the balance of our lives."

Dr. Forrest asked, "You mean in the nature of an annuity?"

"That's what I mean."

Dr. Forrest was thinking, "What could we do with this property way back here in the woods?" Aloud he said, "Where is the property?"

"In Atlanta," was the surprising answer.

"In Atlanta?"

"Yes, sir. Corner of Howard and South Boulevard."

Dr. Forrest thought to himself, "That's a very nice section of Atlanta." He asked, "What kind of property is this?"

"A store. Go down and look at it. See what you can do with it."

Dr. Forrest's curiosity was aroused. The next time he

161

was in Atlanta, he went out to see the property. He found it really in a very nice section, and the store Mr. Earl talked about was an ultra-modern supermarket. The store itself was on the second lot; the corner lot was hard-surfaced for a parking lot for customers.

When Dr. Forrest saw such an elaborate piece of property and remembered the humble home of the Earls, he thought that surely he must have the wrong corner. As soon as possible, he went back to see Mr. Earl and question him.

"That's my store," he answered.

"How did you get a store like that?"

Mr. Earl told him: "I had a little frame building on that lot where the store now stands, and my wife and I carried on a little grocery business there for twenty-eight years. We lived in a room in the back end of the store and saved our money. Finally I put up that building, but I feel that I made a mistake in listening to the real estate men and the builders. They encouraged me to do things I hadn't planned. I had enough money to build a nice store compared to the one I had there; but they over-persuaded me to put in air-conditioning, inbuilt refrigeration, and so many other things that I owe $15,000.00. I'm asking you to take that store and property and pay me so much a month for the rest of my life and the rest of my wife's life."

A certain sum was agreed upon. For a year the Institute kept the property, but found that the rent of four hundred dollars a month was less than the expenses. Thereupon the property was sold for $40,000.00 cash. After the $15,000.00 obligation was paid, there remained somewhat less than $25,000.00 to use for the work of the school. From this sum came the money to build the superstructure and the porches of Earl Hall, the classroom building. The school canteen and bookstore are housed on the first floor, offices and classrooms on the second, and classrooms on the third.

Thus God again honored the prayers of His children.

Only one of the needs mentioned at the beginning of this chapter has not yet been met by God: that of a church building to be used exclusively for religious services. Until the time when that prayer is answered, the students are using the David Ovens Student Center erected in 1951. How lovely it would be, nevertheless, to have a place set apart on the campus exclusively for the worship of the One who has made the Institute possible, the Lord Jesus Christ. Some day, in the providence of God, such a building will be erected as God touches the hearts of His own. It would be fitting to call this sanctuary Forrest Chapel.

Marvelous is the love of God in providing those things for which His children in His will pray. More wonderful still is the fact that He does "exceeding abundantly above" what they ask or think. In the miraculous goodness of God, He fulfilled several of Dr. Forrest's dreams—dreams that, humanly speaking, seemed almost impossible to bring to pass.

The first dream was that of a good road linking the Institute campus with Toccoa. This was completed in 1944.

A second dream was that of owning some beautiful bottom land, rich and fertile, between the Institute and town. This dream also became a reality, and upon this land the dairy barns are built. It is a picturesque sight to see the cattle grazing on the creek banks near the barns.

A third dream came to pass with the purchase of the power plant and water rights to the source of Toccoa Creek, that property excluded in the original purchase. Dr. Forrest had for a long time wanted to buy the plant for use by the school, as their little plant had become inadequate as the school enlarged, but lacked funds to do so.

Meanwhile, the Georgia Power Company had come into Toccoa and was now supplying the power to the city. Dr. Forrest became acquainted with Mr. Preston G. Arkwright, the president of the company. At the time that Dr. Forrest was praying for $15,000.00, the amount necessary to purchase the plant, he decided to call on his friend, Mr. Arkwright. Imagine his surprise when Mr. Arkwright greeted him with the words: "I've been wanting to see you. The Georgia Power Company has asked me to hand you this check as a donation for your work out at the Falls." When he looked at the amount, it was for $15,500.00! The Lord had provided not only the amount needed for the transaction, but had also included the $500.00 necessary for the transfer expense.

The plant was very much run down, actually almost a wreck. Since that time it has been restored and has supplied most of the electricity used on the campus. Within the past two years the plant has been doubled in size and a diesel unit installed, the gift of a former student. A new dam has also been built on the mountain above the power plant to make possible more adequate water storage.

These dreams made reality were, in a sense, "bonuses" given by God to faithful laborers as rewards for duties well done, for lives consecrated to His service, and for prayers and sacrifices made in His work.

Yet it is not to be supposed that there were no "hard spots" during these years. Times of testing prove the worth of a man or a movement. There was, for example, the long period of time when only the hole showed where the classroom building should be; there were months when four and five students lived in a room large enough for only two; and there was the tragedy of the Second World War.

Within three months after the declaration of war, serious inroads had been made into the school. With drives on every hand for defense purposes, donations to the school practically stopped. The students taken by the Government for military and defense purposes cut nearly a thousand dollars a month from the school income; at the same time food costs doubled pre-war prices. For a time the campus looked somewhat like a "Female Academy."

The Institute was making its contributions to the nation during this crisis: many of its former students were placed in responsible positions in the army, the navy, and civilian posts. Girls went to Washington as secretaries and stenographers. And the best part was that most of these young people not only took a job or went to fight on the battle front, but also exerted an influence for Christ wherever they went.

In order to keep operating, the Institute lowered the age for admission and took many younger children who had to be educated away from home. This created some problems, but also the privilege of giving children Christian training and education.

During the war more than five hundred former Toccoa Falls students enlisted, or were drafted, into some branch of service; and as the end of the war came, so also came the problem of taking care of many of these boys who had married and now had families, but who nonetheless wanted to finish their education.

The need for living accommodations for married students constituted just one more opportunity for God to perform another miracle, and He did so. Fifteen comfortable and attractive cottages, each having five rooms, were built on the campus by the Federal Housing Authority; and several trailers were also moved to the campus. These houses and trailers were given outright to the school, to be occupied for the first two years by veteran students. With the houses were supplied the beds, tables, chairs, cooking range, refrigerator, water heater, and even small details such as a waste basket and garbage pail. The trailers also were completely furnished.

While the trailers were more or less temporary means of sheltering students, the houses are still in excellent condition and are used by married students and staff members.

Someone has said: "Expect great things from God; attempt great things for God." This statement well summarizes the attitude of Dr. Forrest and his co-laborers during the fourth decade of the school's existence. Praise God—He never fails! He does the "exceeding abundantly above." To Him be glory!

Chapter Twenty

*"Call unto me, and I will answer thee, and shew thee
great and mighty things, which thou knowest not."*
—JEREMIAH 33:3

IN THE LATTER PART of 1948 Dr. Forrest was faced with two
vitally important problems concerning the future of the
Toccoa Falls Institute. One was the problem of some ac-
cumulating debts, and the other was the possibility for
some kind of endowment.

He recalled the number of times he had been asked how
much endowment Toccoa Falls Institute had. His answer
had always been, "None at all."

The next question was always the same: "How do you
get along without a large endowment? You're just hung up
in space."

He remembered that he invariably answered, "That's
true; we are hung up in space just like the stars, and we
are hung upon the same thing—the faithfulness and care
of our Heavenly Father."

Now he thought, "Does God still want us to hang in
space—or should we try to establish an endowment?"

Then his mind turned to his other great problem. Again
the Institute was in critical need of financial help to erase
debts that had been piling up, many because of the continuous building and maintenance program in a system
so large as this. This time the amount was staggeringly
high—$50,000.00 to clear the slate—and no apparent way

of getting it. The policy of the school had always been not to take an offering for Toccoa Falls and not to beg people for money. Tell them what was being done and trust that God would speak to their hearts about giving.

On this occasion the amount seemed so staggering that he was utterly at a loss to know what to do.

In the meantime a certain piece of property right in the heart of the city of Toccoa attracted his attention. Again and again he thought, "Wouldn't it be nice if the Institute owned that block and had a row of stores built there as a permanent endowment for the school?"

So a little cautious inquiry was made. Dr. Forrest discovered that the property belonged to the Southern Railway Company. It was the north half of a whole block given to the company some seventy years before when they were first building their tracks through the town. The tracks and the railroad station and platforms occupied half of the block; the other half, fronting upon the main street of the town, was left standing alone, grown up in weeds and brush and used as a scrap heap, although it was a most valuable site for stores and business houses. Dr. Forrest was told that when three old gentlemen gave this property to the Railroad, they had placed a reversion clause in the deed which said that the land must be used for railroad purposes only. Therefore, it could not be bought by anybody or used by anybody except for such purposes.

Dr. Forrest thought, "Well, that's that," but every time he went to town he saw that lot. Each time he saw it, he desired it more than before. Finally a conviction was born that God wanted the school to have that piece of property.

At length, it occurred to him that he'd better go talk to the Southern Railway Company's attorney, Judge Wheeler, whose home and office were in Gainesville, Georgia, forty miles away. When Dr. Forrest told him what he wanted, Judge Wheeler looked up and said, "Doc, I wish you could get it, but you can't. Dozens of men have been wanting to buy that piece of property. It's the most valuable piece of property for its size in Stephens County; but it can't be bought, unless you were going to use it for the Southern Railway Company."

Dr. Forrest challenged him: "Judge, who said it can't be bought?"

"Well," he replied, "the reversion clause is in the deed."

"Have you ever seen it?"

"No, but I know it's there."

"Do you know anybody else who's ever seen it?"

"No, but—." He interrupted himself: "Listen, what do you want me to do, look it up?"

Dr. Forrest grinned. "I wish you would, just on general principles. If you find it there, I'll pay you for the time; if you don't find it there, it costs me nothing."

"Fair enough," was the answer.

In about two weeks Judge Wheeler called Dr. Forrest on the phone and said, "Come on down; I want to show you something."

Dr. Forrest went down. When the judge saw him, he said, "Look here, the reversion clause is there all right, but it doesn't mention the Southern Railway; it says this property must be used for public welfare, and that's right up your alley. Public welfare—therefore the school *can* buy it, whereas no other individual could buy it for personal gain." He concluded, "I think you'd better go to Washington and talk to the Southern Railway men about it." Dr. Forrest thought so, too.

When he walked into the office of one of the vice-presidents who had to do with real estate interests of the railway company, the vice-president looked startled. He and Dr. Forrest had known each other for a long time, so recognized each other at once. "Why, Doc, whatever brought you to Washington today?"

"Oh," Dr. Forrest responded, "you wouldn't know if I told you. The Lord sent me up here today."

Without a smile the man answered, "I believe you're right. Sit down."

He continued: "You've come to see about that piece of property in Toccoa, haven't you? Yesterday my office was full of the big brass of the Southern Railway System talking about that piece of property and the fact that you wanted it. Doc, we can't hand you that land on a platter. We'd like to see you have it, but we can't do that. Our directors would climb all over us."

Dr. Forrest interrupted him: "Nobody asked you to do that."

He asked, "Do you know how much that property's worth?"

"Well, in Toccoa it's appraised at $40,000.00."

"Our appraisal's $50,000.00. We can't just hand it to you."

Again Dr. Forrest remonstrated: "Nobody's asked you to hand it to us on a platter. Sell it to us. We'll give you $5,000.00 for it. You've held that land for seventy-five years; it's never brought you one dime. You've been paying taxes on it all that time and getting nothing in return. Want to keep it and pay taxes for seventy more years? Nobody else can buy it but us, and it'll do us a lot of good."

"By George, I believe we'll take you up on that."

Dr. Forrest replied, "That's fine; I appreciate it."

He returned home, and by the end of the next week sent a check for $5,000.00. In return, the officials at Washington sent him a quitclaim deed to the property.

Two thousand dollars of this money was the Forrests' personal savings, accumulated bit by bit over a period of twenty years or more. But that was all they had. The school had no money. At this time it occurred to Dr. Forrest to write a letter to a friend of his who had frequently helped the school, Mr. Frank B. Huston, who spends his summers in Asheville, North Carolina, and his winters in Columbia, South Carolina. Dr. Forrest wrote Mr. Huston and told him about the matter. By return mail there came $3,000.00 from him. Thus was the money obtained to send to Washington.

The railway officials then asked, "What are you going to do with this property?"

"We want to build a row of stores on it as a permanent endowment for the school."

"Do you have anything in sight for it?"

"I have found, upon a little inquiry, that an insurance company would lend us money to build the stores, with the property and the stores as security for the money."

The answer was disquieting: "You're building up trouble for yourself, very definitely."

"What do you mean?"

"Well, what you're planning to do will make the property very, very valuable. Then, when that time comes, you'll find the heirs of these three old men coming around wanting their share, even though everything's been legal. I'm afraid you'll find yourself under constant lawsuits, maybe for years to come. The advice of the Southern Railroad is that you sell the property and use the proceeds for the school."

Dr. Forrest had planned further ahead than these men realized, though. He was able to meet their objections. "Now, we've gotten ready for that. I've already been to see the heirs of all three of these old men. Mr. Sage had two living heirs, two sons, both of whom are past eighty years of age. One of them was in the hospital when I called on him and has since died. I got a quitclaim deed from each of them. Mr. Doyle had five living heirs, most of whom settled around Seneca, South Carolina. I got a quitclaim deed from each of them. We never could find any heirs of Mr. Alexander, but in lieu of a quitclaim deed, in that case, we got an order from the State Supreme Court which would supersede any kind of claim."

"You've planned well; you're in the clear; go ahead. The property is now yours to be used to the best advantage for the school."

Then Dr. Forrest began to think about paying back the money that they'd have to borrow for the buildings. He thought about the taxes to pay. While Toccoa Falls Institute is free from tax, a proposition like that up in the town, not on the school campus, but as a matter of income, would be taxed. He thought of the insurance to pay. He thought of the upkeep of the property and the possibility of men getting in there to sell things that his conscience wouldn't allow to be sold on property belonging to the school.

His conclusion was that he wasn't in the real estate business after all; but in school business. He decided to take the advice of the Southern Railroad officials to sell and quietly let the word out that the property could be purchased. Within a week $50,000.00 cash had been offered for the property. On the very day that the Board of Trustees had given consent to sell, a second man walked into Dr. Forrest's office with a cashier's check for $50,000.00 in his pocket. He, too, had wished to purchase the land.

Once more the Heavenly Father manifested His tender care for the school; and after much prayer, Dr. Forrest and the other school authorities felt that it was God's leading that the money obtained from the sale of this property be used to pay debts and put the school on a sound financial basis.

Chapter Twenty-one

"I will trust, and not be afraid."—ISAIAH 12:2

THERE HAVE BEEN many wonderful miracles in the way of providential care at Toccoa Falls Institute and Bible College since it was organized forty-five years ago, but one of the most spectacular and wonderful miracles witnessed during the school's existence took place after the disastrous fire destroyed LeTourneau Hall, the largest and best building on the grounds, on August 3, 1950.

It was Thursday evening, about seven-thirty. The day had been lovely, albeit a busy one. A new dish washer had been installed in the kitchen of LeTourneau Hall; blankets, sheets, and commencement robes had been transferred from another building to Room 6, recently set aside as a new storeroom; and several of the girls had just left for Christian service in a neighboring town. Dr. Forrest was preaching in Roanoke, Virginia; Mr. Barnes was on his way to Atlanta to catch a plane for Miami. The delegates to the American Sunday School Union Convention were in the chapel, raising their voices in songs of praise to God. Students and staff members were waiting for the bell to call them in to evening study hall.

One of the teachers was leisurely sauntering back from a visit to Trailer Court. Suddenly he noticed smoke rising from the roof above the guest room in LeTourneau Hall. In a second the horrifying truth that the building was afire smote him; he broke into a run and came and began to ring the bell violently, bringing everybody out of the chapel and from their other duties.

Although everyone, including the fire department from Toccoa, fought courageously to put out the fire and at one time seemed to have it under control, the flames sprang up again and finally forced the firefighters to abandon their efforts to save the building. Thereupon they immediately turned their attention to rescuing as much as possible. However, because the building was finished in pine paneling, the fire spread rapidly, quickly forcing everyone outside. Within an hour and a half of the discovery of the fire, the fourth wall slid into the burning inferno, carrying with it the porch on which was inscribed the school motto, "Where Character Is Developed With Intellect." One of the pillars teetered, then straightened upright. LeTourneau Hall was no more.

God performed miracles, nevertheless, even during the fire. Since the buildings on the campus are close together, only God could have kept other buildings from burning at the same time. This He did.

How did Dr. Forrest feel when he heard about the disaster which had befallen his beloved school? His faith was not daunted, but increased in the God to whom he looks for every need. This is his own version of what took place that night, August 3, 1950:

"I was preaching in Roanoke, Virginia, that night in a large Methodist Church. My text was 'I will trust, and not be afraid.' We had a great service. People were talking to me about how much encouragement that message had given them and how they felt now that they could stand up against difficulties and trials.

"When I went back to the hotel where I was staying, they told me somebody was trying to get me long distance from Georgia. I wasn't surprised at that because it frequently happens when I'm away from home. Finally I went to my room; and when I picked up the telephone and made the contact, it was Kelly Barnes, the superintendent, telling me, 'Dad, I'm most terribly sorry to tell you, but LeTourneau Hall has burned to the ground tonight and is a total loss. You had better come home.'

"The first reaction I had after the stunning blow subsided was to think, 'Look here, old man, you'd better begin to practice what you preach.'

"I had just been telling other people that when difficult times come, pressures come, disappointments come, we must not be fearful—we must trust and believe. I had been telling them that God would take care of them; and now I must take the same message to myself. I got down on my knees in my room there in the hotel that night and spread the matter before the Lord. This was our largest building—our best building—there were more than forty girls staying in that building. In addition to that, our gymnasium was there, a beautiful room which we also used as an auditorium for special services when our chapel was too small. Our dining room was in the same building and also our kitchen. I knew that all this dormitory space, the beautiful gym with all its trimmings and equipment, the dining room chairs, tables, dishes, silverware, cooking utensils, about four tons of food, and so many things, including the storage of our commencement robes and all such equipment, were completely destroyed. I confess that when I thought about it, it was a paralyzing thought.

"But now I began to drink from our heavenly fountain of courage and faith, confidence and trust—and it took away my fear.

"I knew it would require at least $100,000, perhaps more, to replace that building; indeed, it would cost about $150,000 for us to replace it; and I did not have the least idea, humanly speaking, how we could get that money, or where. But I knew God knew."

Of course, the entire student family was equally stunned. Summer school was in session; the school was entertaining an American Sunday School Union Conference on the grounds and there were nearly two hundred people to be fed; two weeks later more than one hundred young people of The Christian and Missionary Alliance, from all the southeastern states, were due on the campus for a week's conference. Could rooms be found for everyone? Where could the food be cooked and served? How could everything be managed?

Fortunately, all beds on the campus had been made up before the conference, but not all were in use. Therefore, all persons who had lived in LeTourneau Hall were provided living accommodations before bedtime the night of the fire. At six o'clock the next morning the school bell rang as usual; breakfast was right on time at seven. Food was prepared under some difficulties in the home economics department in Gate Cottage, where there were several electric ranges and a few odds and ends in the way of cooking utensils. Somebody hurried to town and got paper plates, cups, spoons, and forks, and some food; and breakfast—consisting of bacon and eggs, coffee, bread, and oranges—was served cafeteria fashion, everybody standing up to eat. In fact, matters ran along like this for several weeks, with the exception that tables were set up, people eating in relays.

Within a month a temporary dining room and a kitchen, which were used for nearly two years, were set up in a building that had been started to be used for a warehouse. At the time of the fire the framework was up, but there was no roof and no cement floor. The floor space was nearly the same as that of the dining room which had burned. A "lean-to" was built on either side, one for a kitchen, the other for a storeroom. By the time school opened, September 5, the building was ready for occupancy, although not finished. At first students could look through the walls as they ate; but soon siding was put on the building and gas heaters were installed, making the place comfortable for winter weather.

Now, what could be done for the money to replace LeTourneau Hall? This was an absolute necessity. The school authorities felt they could not stop—they must go on. Students came for the opening of the fall term just as though nothing had happened. They were taken care of in the very best way possible; but they were scattered around the campus, crowded uncomfortably. Still they came—and stayed—and the school went right on.

The first thing that happened in the way of the supply of funds for a new building came from the county in which Toccoa Falls Institute is situated—Stephens County, Georgia. Neighbors and friends of the school got together, formed a committee, selected a local businessman (Mr. Ray Trogdon) as chairman, and finally came and handed Dr. Forrest $28,000.00 to start a building fund. This was particularly encouraging because it came from neighbors and from the community round about. It was a wonderful testimonial to the value of the school and showed how the neighbors felt and thought about it and the esteem in which they held Dr. Forrest.

Finally, by means of mail and friends around the earth, the funds grew to $62,000.00, but it was decided not to begin serious building operations until there was at least $100,000.00 in cash on hand. Where could the remaining $40,000.00 be obtained? No one could imagine.

It was at this time that Dr. Forrest was called to New York City to attend a meeting of the Board of Managers of The Christian and Missionary Alliance. While he was there, the telephone rang in his office at Tococa Falls one morning. When told by his secretary that Dr. Forrest was in New York City that day, the friend who was trying to get in touch with him contacted him there. This friend was Mr. Tom Glasgow, a very prominent and well-known businessman of Charlotte, North Carolina. In some way or other he had heard about the fire and had earnestly been praying that God bestow supernatural help.

About five years before, Dr. Forrest had had the privilege of speaking to the Men's Club of a large Presbyterian Church in Charlotte, and God had made him a blessing to Mr. Glasgow. In return, Mr. Glasgow wanted to do something for Toccoa Falls. He contacted a friend of his in Charlotte, a very prominent businessman. Indeed, he is well known as a merchant prince in that great city—the man who built the famous Ivey Store there. He is a man of rare ability, a Canadian by birth, member of a Presbyterian church of Charlotte, and a man who had made a great deal of money and was very generous and anxious to help in any way he could. He was the main supporter of several musical organizations and other groups of culture, entertainment, and benefit for the city.

Tom Glasgow thought about this friend of his and contacted him and told him about the need at Toccoa Falls. This friend, Mr. David Ovens, became very much interested. He was interested first because of his sincere friendship and confidence in Mr. Glasgow. Too, he was interested in finding ways and means of doing the most he could with his money. At any rate, he told Mr. Glasgow to have Dr. Forrest come to see him. Mr. Glasgow felt this invitation to be of so great importance that, when he contacted Dr. Forrest in New York and told him to be sure to stop in Charlotte on the way home, he added, "And I don't mean maybe!"

When Dr. Forrest arrived, he was met at the station by Mr. Glasgow, who took him to his office. From there he called Mr. David Ovens' office, only to hear that Mr. Ovens had come to work that morning feeling very weak and ill and had utterly collapsed. They had had to take him back home. "Well," Dr. Forrest thought, "that's the end of that."

However, some days later Mr. Ovens asked that Dr. Forrest write a letter telling him what he was doing and what he wanted to do. The letter was written. In a few days Mr. Ovens called Mr. Glasgow and told him that he wanted to see Dr. Forrest. As he put it: "I can't get that man Forrest out of my hair."

Mr. Glasgow again called Toccoa Falls. This time Dr. Forrest happened to be at home. He immediately went back to Charlotte, to see Mr. Glasgow and to contact Mr. Ovens, whom he had never met personally.

This time Mr. Ovens was able to see him. When Dr. Forrest entered his office, he found himself in the midst of splendor. A beautifully appointed office it was, everything appearing to be just exactly right, everything made to suit everything else. Mr. Ovens looked very small in his chair behind his desk in that great office, but there was a strength —something about the look in his eyes—that made one feel like paying strict attention to what he might have to say.

His very first remark to Dr. Forrest was startling. He said, "Tom Glasgow has interested me in what you're doing over there in Georgia, and I believe God wants me to do something about it."

Dr. Forrest was staggered. He did not know what to say in return. Finally Mr. Ovens called for somebody outside, and a nice looking gentleman came in. Mr. Ovens said, "This is Mr. Powell. He looks after my financial interests." Turning to Mr. Powell, he continued, "Powell, what did you do with those securities that I gave you to send to Dr. Forrest at Toccoa Falls, Georgia?"

Mr. Powell answered, "Mr. Ovens, those securities are down in the bank being prepared to mail to him tonight."

Mr. Ovens asked, "Powell, how much are those securities worth?"

Dr. Forrest tried to keep what they call a "poker" face, whatever that is, but he nearly fell out of his chair when Mr. Powell replied, "Mr. Ovens, they're worth $40,000.00."

Mr. Ovens looked at Dr. Forrest, grinned, and said, "Doctor, will that help you a little?"

Dr. Forrest stammered, "I don't know what to say. Did he say $4,000.00 or $40,000.00?"

He answered, "I think he said $40,000.00." Then he turned to Mr. Powell: "Powell, you'd better put your hat and coat on and go down to the bank and get that stuff. Indeed, you might take Dr. Forrest with you."

When they got that "stuff," Dr. Forrest found it to be high grade securities, which were afterwards sold for more than $40,000.00. Can you imagine how he felt? Can you imagine how it humbled him? Can you imagine how grateful he was?

He went back to see Mr. Ovens and thank him. At this time Mr. Ovens said, "You know, I feel very happy about this matter because I feel that for one time in my life I have done something because God told me to do it, and you're more than welcome to this money. However, if you had come to my office and asked me for $40,000.00, I think I'd have thrown you out; but when Tom Glasgow told me about your work and what you are trying to do in developing young men and women for fruitful service and life, it was impressed upon me, I believe from God Himself, that I should help you. That's the reason why I did it."

He went on: "In fact, last Sunday morning I woke feeling so bad I was afraid I was going to die. I was so anxious that you should get this help that I felt like calling for my attorney to come to my house right then to put a codicil to my will so that if I should die before seeing you, you would still get this money."

Of this miracle Dr. Forrest says: "Could that be anything else but an answer to prayer? Surely you will agree with me it was and was one more evidence of the tender thoughtfulness of our Lord. How He could speak to a man in Charlotte—a man whom I had never before seen and to whom I had never talked—and tell him what he should do! But we had our hundred thousand dollars and were prepared to go along."

The other money came in from time to time until really during the next two years two buildings were erected. The building that burned was replaced on the same foundation; only this time it is a thoroughly fireproof building, built entirely of steel, concrete, brick, and tile. The only things wood about the building are the outside doors. At that time steel doors were unobtainable, but some day the wood doors will be replaced by steel ones. The building now is standing—a monument to the care and the providence and the love of our Heavenly Father.

The new LeTourneau Hall is a beautiful structure, with enough dormitory space to house ninety-six girls, plus four large guest rooms with private baths. These rooms are built around a large and beautifully appointed lounge or reception room. On the first floor of the building is the largest and one of the loveliest dining rooms in northeast Georgia, with a fine kitchen adjoining it. It is a building of which to be justly proud and for which no apologies need be made to anyone.

Every time any of the staff go into LeTourneau Hall and look at the pictures of Mr. Ovens and Mr. Glasgow on the walls of the foyer, thanks is given to God that these men ever lived and that their ears were attuned to their Heavenly Father and their hearts anxious to do His bidding.

In addition to the replacement of LeTourneau Hall, there has also been erected on the campus a beautiful cement block building which houses the gymnasium and several other departments of the work. The gymnasium floor is sixty by one hundred feet. At one end of the gymnasium is a beautiful stage with large, luxurious blue velour curtains and everything properly appointed. The main portion of the gymnasium will seat several hundred people, and in the bleacher seats on both sides of the main floor some hundreds can be seated. All the larger services and exercises are held in this building. It is the headquarters for the speech department; and the stage is especially adapted for drama, plays, pageants, and various entertainment features of this department, to say nothing of the Sunday services and special occasions of all kinds. It's a thing of beauty, that building, and those who live at Toccoa Falls never cease to be thankful for it.

In this same building is the newest department on the campus—the department of radio technique. A sound-proof room has been finished in one corner of the building, and the students are taught how to build a radio projector and transmitter, to say nothing of the receiving sets. This department is designed especially for the men and women who are going to the mission field. In these days when so many mission fields are being closed to American missionaries, the air is still carrying the message of the Gospel from radio stations scattered throughout the world. How wonderful it will be to send young men to the mission field—young men who know how to build a mission station for themselves after they get there.

The band room is upstairs in another corner of this much used building; while still another room has been equipped for teaching students to play the Hammond electric organ. A room under the bleachers is equipped for games, such as ping-pong and shuffleboard. The staff room of the school annual and dark rooms occupy one of the sections upstairs. In this one building alone students can receive quite a liberal education.

One never ceases to thrill to the atmosphere of the building on Sunday morning when the Institute family gathers for its Sunday service. Nobody's ever complained to the students about talking or giggling when they go into that place for services. Somehow it's natural for them to be quiet. They sit in meditation, waiting for time for the service to begin. There's a real upsurge of joy and praise when the beautiful velour curtains are drawn aside, revealing the choir of thirty to forty voices ready to begin their praises to God. Then the organist begins to play some devotional hymn. *Sing praises to God.*

Each time a service is held in this building, there is the spoken or unspoken thought: "If only Mr. Ovens could be here to see this." The building has been named "The David Ovens Student Center." How happy he would be if he were able to come to see it, and how grateful the Institute family is for it!

So this is one more of the miracles that have been occurring over and over again in the last forty-five years, since the time Dr. Forrest made the down payment of ten dollars on the original property. It has grown since then to something in excess of one million dollars, every bit of which is attributed to the tender care and providence of the Heavenly Father, because the work is done in His fear and seeking only His favor and His blessing.

Chapter Twenty-two

"Having therefore obtained help of God, I continue unto this day, witnessing both to small and great."—Acts 26:22a

MOST MEN WOULD count one field of endeavor—one life occupation—to be sufficient. To the majority, the founding and running of a Bible school on faith would be not only a full, but an overwhelming task; not so with Dr. Forrest. He has labored as a full-time minister, as a full-time school man, as a national leader in two denominations, and as a full-time evangelist. Few persons can encompass so much in one life-time. Yet, with all his multitudinous duties, he has never lost sight of the individual. One of his greatest joys has always been the leading of an individual soul to Christ. Whether at the altar rail, in a train, on the street, or in a home—he has remembered the commandment of the Lord: *Ye have not chosen me, but I have chosen you and ordained you, that ye should bring forth fruit, and that your fruit should remain, and whatsoever ye shall ask of the father in my name, he will give it you.*

Of this verse and of personal soul-winning, Dr. Forrest has said:

"This verse takes in every believing child of God, not just ministers. Now to preach the Gospel from the pulpit is a great privilege. I have had this privilege for more than half a century and have tried my best to preach the Gospel around the world. Sometimes friends have, in their kindness, told me how they envied me the privilege of being a minister and seeing people

184

brought to a saving knowledge of the Lord Jesus Christ. My answer to that always has been that some of the most beautiful experiences I've had in leading souls to Christ have been when I have done so face to face and man to man, in what we call 'personal work.' The humblest child of God is privileged to do this kind of service."

Dr. Forrest's whole ministry can be epitomized in his love for the soul of the individual. For this reason he has left his lovely wife alone much of their married life to go out in evangelistic work; for this reason he has developed a Bible school to train others in the art of soul-winning; and for this reason he knows no rich nor poor, no great nor small as he greets the man, the woman, the boy, the girl in the everyday walk of life. It should prove challenging to all to become acquainted with a few of his experiences as he has touched shoulders with all types of people and made Christ known to some whom others might call "impossible."

Consider, for example, the drunkard he met in St. Louis some years ago. Rev. Paul Rader, president of The Christian and Missionary Alliance, had planned a big evangelistic campaign in that city. A board tabernacle, seating about two thousand, had been erected especially for the meetings. At the last moment, Rev. Rader couldn't go; he wired Dr. Forrest, insisting that he take his place and send a picture of himself to bill the place and advertise the meetings. As Dr. Forrest had no recent picture, he had to have one made. While the photographer was taking pictures, Dr. Forrest told him a funny story. As they laughed uproariously, the photographer snapped the shutter. Dr. Forrest was grinning so broadly that fourteen of his teeth showed. He enclosed the grinning photograph with the others as a joke. Imagine his amazement and chagrin when he arrived in St. Louis and found that that was the photograph that was being used. Everywhere he turned, he looked at that grin. It looked more like a comedian than a preacher. Ten thousand little hand cards had been printed, a blotter on one side and that grin on the other, along with the hour of the service and the place of meeting. These had been distributed all over town. Larger posters were on fences and telephone poles and everywhere one could be tacked up for blocks and blocks around the place where the services were to be held.

One day while in St. Louis, Dr. Forrest had occasion to go down town—to a bed company that made pushback beds such as were used at that time in Stewart Dormitory. When he got off the trolley car at the nearest point to the plant, he noticed a fellow wrapped around the lamp post on the corner. Seeing that the man was drunk, he walked right on by, only to hear him call, "Shay, wait a minute."

Dr. Forrest didn't want to stay there and get mixed up with a drunkard, so he took a few more steps. But the man called again, "Wait a minute. Please. I beg you, wait a minute. I know you."

Dr. Forrest can never resist the plea of a person who seems in distress. He went back, thinking he might help the man. As he approached, the drunkard drawled, "I knowed you the minute you got off that car."

"You don't know me."

"Yesh, I do. I have your pikshur right here in my pocket." He pulled out one of those little hand blotters with that grin on it. Dr. Forrest was so surprised to see it that he didn't know what to say. The drunkard continued: "Shay, I want to ashk you a queshun. I want to ashk you if you'll tell me how to be happy like that, becaush I'm miserable."

Dr. Forrest talked to him for a while, but he was so drunk he couldn't understand much. Finally Dr. Forrest said, "Where do you live?" The fellow told him, but he didn't know much about the streets, so he said, "If you'll show me how to get you there, pal, I'll take you home."

"I sho wou' appreshate it."

Dr. Forrest unfolded him from around the lamp post and wrapped him around himself and started off. He almost carried the man for two or three blocks. When they came to his house, Dr. Forrest knocked on the door. A nice looking lady answered the knock. She was the man's wife and was humiliated by his condition. In the meantime, he'd slumped down on the steps. Between them, they got him onto his feet, into the house, and on into the parlor.

Dr. Forrest sat down and began to talk with the two of them. As the conversation continued, the man sobered. Dr. Forrest took a Testament out of his pocket and read passages to him, talked with him, and prayed with him. That man accepted Christ right there. Because he'd been so drunk, Dr. Forrest couldn't put too much dependence in his conversion; however, he did know that the man was sober and seemed to mean what he said. The wife was in a paroxysm of tears most of the time. She was ashamed and also hopeful; she was already a Christian. It was pathetic to see her and hear what she said.

Dr. Forrest went on his way. About two years afterward he was back in St. Louis and had occasion to go to that same bed factory. When he alighted from the car at that corner, he couldn't help remembering the last time he'd been there. He looked at the lamp post and by impulse decided he'd go find out how that drunken fellow ever got along. He still didn't know the street or number; but after half carrying the man home, he surely did know how to get there.

He found the place and knocked; and the same lady came to the door. She knew him instantly. "Oh," she cried, "there's nobody in the world I'd rather see. Come in."

As they entered the parlor, she said, "I want to show you something." She pointed to that little blotter with that silly grin propped up against the clock on the mantle.

"Oh," remonstrated Dr. Forrest, "you don't want that."

She disagreed. "My husband wouldn't take anything for that."

"Why, you don't want a grinning comedian like that."

"Grinning nothing. That's what attracted my husband to you. He wanted to be happy that way himself."

"Well, what became of him?"

"What became of him! Oh, I wish he were coming home now. Can't you stay until he gets home? He's a happy Christian. He was saved that day. He's never touched a drop of liquor since, and he works down at the city mission. He tells other men how to be happy."

The child of God should seek every available opportunity to witness to others for Christ. Dr. Forrest often finds his opening in casual conversation. The following incident illustrates this.

Dr. Forrest was traveling to an engagement by pullman. While the porter was making up the berths, he had to go to what is called the smoking room. A fellow was in there about half-drunk. He offered Dr. Forrest a drink of whiskey. When the drink was refused, he kept insisting. To avoid him Dr. Forrest went back to his berth. The night was terribly hot. He sat down to take off his shoes, and lo and behold, in came the drunkard—and his berth was right opposite. He sat down, remarking to Dr. Forrest: "Hot as hell, ain't it?"

"No, sir."

"Doncha think it's hot?"

"It's pretty hot, my friend, but not anything like as hot as hell."

"Jush whudda ya mean by that?"

Dr. Forrest had his opening. He began to talk to the

man, and finally went over and sat down beside him on the edge of his berth. At length the fellow said, "You know, I've had lots of folks tell me what a fool I am to get drunk, but I've never had one talk to me this way. Nobody's talked to me like this since my mother died. She used to tell me how foolish it was. I don't know who you are or what you are, but I wish I could quit drinking."

Dr. Forrest told him that there wasn't any trouble about quitting drinking if he'd get saved—that'd take care of the drinking and everything else with it. He talked for a long time; finally he put the man to bed and sat on the edge of his berth and prayed for him. The fellow felt around until he got to Dr. Forrest's hand and kept squeezing it during the prayer. He prayed under his breath for himself, too. At last Dr. Forrest left him and went to bed.

The next morning Dr. Forrest was in the wash room shaving. In the mirror he saw the man come in behind him and look all around. Finally he spotted him. He said, "You know, I still don't know who you are or what you are, but God heard my prayer last night after you left, and I'm going home a brand new man," and he did. Dr. Forrest heard from him many times after that.

One of Dr. Forrest's joys consists in baptizing those whose testimony assures him that they are sons of God. One of these occasions was most unusual.

Some years ago a letter came to Dr. Forrest from the superintendent of the home missions for the Synod of Georgia (Presbyterian) telling of an old mountaineer up in Rabun County who had been converted and wanted to join the Presbyterian Church. Since he wanted to be immersed, would Dr. Forrest, as pastor of the First Presbyterian Church of Toccoa, go up there and do it? He replied at once that he would be very happy to go and baptize the old gentleman on the first opportunity.

Finally the day came. When Dr. Forrest reached the

neighborhood where the old man lived, he found a great deal of interest. Quite a large group of people had gathered by the side of the stream where a place had been dug out deep enough for the occasion.

The old man who was to be baptized was afraid he was being a nuisance and worrying everyone by insisting upon immersion, but Dr. Forrest hastened to assure him that he was not worried at all but, to the contrary, would be very happy to baptize him if he knew why he was being baptized.

He answered, "Yessir, I think I do." Then he told his experience. He was a man then rapidly approaching middle life. He had heavy whiskers which grew close up under his eyes; and when his hat brim was pulled down, those black eyes looked almost like guns being pointed at one. He looked so as he began speaking.

He said, "I was a terrible fella to make likker and a terrible fella to drink likker and I was a terrible fella to cuss. I couldn't talk to nobody without cussin'. And then I got to thinkin' about my boys. They had begun to drink the likker I wuz makin' and in fact, one of them right now is in the penitencheeary, and I said to myself, sez I, 'This ain't no way to bring these boys up, this ain't no way fer you to live yourself,' and I got to thinkin' about it more 'n' more. I tried to quit makin' likker and I tried to quit drinkin' it and I tried to quit cussin', but all the time I found myself gettin' weaker 'n' weaker. I broke down over 'n' over again. I thought there wuzn't no other way fer me to make a livin' except makin' likker, and I drank it becuz I jes' wanted to, and things wa'nt goin' well a tall with me or with the family.

"Finally, I began to think about God and wondered if God would help a man like me, and one day I went down right behind that patch o' timber, and I got down behind a tree, and I cried to Almighty God and told Him how I'd tried to quit makin' likker and I'd tried to quit drinkin' it and I'd tried to quit cussin' and how helpless I wuz. And you know, Preacher, somehow while I wuz a-prayin', I had a feelin' that God Almighty had heard my prayer, and that He would help me to do whut I couldn't do myself and I felt that God wuz right thar along side o' me. I felt I could almost touch Him, and sure I could speak to Him, and I wuz a-speakin' to Him an' I felt like He wuz a-lissenin' to whut I had to say."

The old man's eyes then grew soft and tender. He said, "Preacher, that wuz nigh onto four year ago; yet I'm glad to tell you, Preacher, that frum that day to this, I ain't tetched a drap o' likker and I ain't cussed a cuss."

Dr. Forrest said, "Mr. Keener, you're ready to be baptized, and I'm ready to baptize you." He went down into the stream and put the old man under the water in the name of the Lord. He had to put him down a second time to get those whiskers under, but a happier man you could not imagine than that old man as he came up out of that hole in the creek. He had followed his Lord in obedience. Later he was made an elder in the Presbyterian Church. His testimony spread through the mountains all round about. Everybody knew that Jim Keener was a man of God.

Men from all walks of life have called upon Dr. Forrest to help them in time of difficulty. The problems have been as diverse as possible. Christians, as well as the unsaved, have looked to him for prayer and help. Always has he sought the answer from God; and God has been pleased to honor his dependence upon Him.

On one of these occasions Dr. Forrest had been conducting a series of meetings in the Presbyterian Church in Gaffney, South Carolina. The services had been good; the results had been wonderful. After the service which had closed the meetings, Dr. Forrest went to his hotel room and retired. He had spoken four times on that Sunday and consequently was very tired. Before he had gotten to sleep, however, the telephone rang. He answered wearily, to hear one of the elders in the church ask, "Could I talk to you for a few minutes if I'd come up to your room?"

Sensing that the man had a need, Dr. Forrest invited him to "come on up."

The man did indeed have a problem. He was the superintendent of a large cotton mill there. His mill was in the grip of a strike that had gone on for many months. People were suffering, and though they'd tried again and again, they could not break the strike. He said, "Tomorrow there will be twenty-nine men meeting me in my office. We want to end this strike, and I want you to go down and talk to those men in my office and help us."

Dr. Forrest demurred, "Wait a minute. I don't want to get mixed up with strikers."

"I believe you'd enjoy doing it," was the odd reply.

"O K., I'll be there at nine o'clock."

At nine the next morning Dr. Forrest went down to the mill office. There were the pickets at the entrance to the mill, marching back and forth. When he arrived, he noticed that the twenty-nine men had increased to about forty—men who wanted to go back to work but couldn't. The superintendent talked to them a little while about the strike, why it came, and so forth. Then he asked Dr. Forrest to say something.

At the conclusion of these remarks, the superintendent asked, "Will you pray for us?"

"Surely."

It was the grimmest kind of meeting—everybody there looked so serious that Dr. Forrest was really frightened. The men rose to their feet; some of them were wearing hats —they removed them. Dr. Forrest prayed, and one or two of the men said "Amen" when he finished.

The superintendent said, "Let's go."

He and Dr. Forrest led the procession out of that office and across the street to the mill yard. Every picket stopped in his tracks as if he were frozen, and there wasn't a sound but the shuffling of men's feet on the road as the forty men crossed it. They went into the mill gate—and no man raised a finger! They went on in silence into the mill, the superintendent pressed a button, the machinery started, and the strike was over. There has not been a strike since. To the contrary, there are now three eight-hour shifts a day there.

In the spring of 1954 a need arose at Toccoa Falls for a car in which the Institute quartet and their leader could make their summer tour. The same superintendent had no way of knowing this need, as no one had been notified of it. Yet one day he telephoned Dr. Forrest and said, "I've been thinking so much about you lately; I can't get you off my mind."

Dr. Forrest chuckled, "That's good."

"I don't have any money to send you, but I have a car here. I was wondering if you could use it. I bought a new one and was going to turn in this one; and I don't know why, but the thought occurred to me that in place of turning it in on the new car, I might give it to you. Do you have any use for it? It's in good condition and will go thousands of miles yet."

Dr. Forrest said, "We need a car right now," and he told him of the need.

"Well, it's your car. Send somebody up for it."

Gratefully was a driver sent for the car. Since it hadn't been used for some time, the tires were dry-rotted. The donor paid for new tires, too.

In his letter to the Galatians, Paul wrote: *Brethren, if a man be overtaken in a fault, ye which are spiritual, restore such an one in the spirit of meekness.* In his years of ministry Dr. Forrest has helped many Christians who were out of fellowship with the Lord back into paths of righteousness and spiritual living. One such incident took place some years ago.

Dr. Forrest had been asked to attend and speak in a missionary conference to be held in a large city in Alabama. Just before leaving Toccoa, he was asked by one of the elders of his church to go see a friend of his who was very ill in a hospital of this Alabama city.

"I'll be happy to go see your friend," Dr. Forrest told the elder.

When he entered the hospital room, Dr. Forrest found a very interesting character. "I wish you could help me," he said, "but after you hear how I've failed God, I'm afraid you'll feel there's no hope for me—either spiritually or physically."

"It seems to me that you're trying to limit God, my friend," Dr. Forrest responded. "Suppose you tell me why you've made such a drastic statement."

Seeming eager to do so, the man told the following unusual story. "I'm a native of Alabama and started in business in this state. However, a number of years ago my wife and I decided to move to Miami, where I also had a successful business. Then my friends became interested in buying and selling land. They told me that there were tremendous possibilities for becoming rich. I decided I'd enter the game and did so. To my amazement and delight I found myself making money 'hand over fist.' These were the days of the Florida land boom in the late twenties.

"At home I had been a Christian man, quite active in Sunday-school work and in other departments of the church. However, when I began to make money so rapidly, I was swept off my feet. The first thing I knew I was buying and selling land on Sunday the same as on any other day. I neglected my church, my Sunday school, and all my other Christian activities—I was so enamored over the idea

194

of becoming rich. Apparently I was succeeding in doing this.

"Finally a little baby boy was given to my wife and me. We had been married for seven years without any children; and when this baby came, I was beside myself with joy. I thought I had received the last touch possible for any man: I was becoming rich and now had an heir.

"When the baby was only a few weeks old, however, he became ill. He grew worse and worse until finally we took him to the hospital for expert care. Nevertheless, he continued to grow worse until he scarcely resembled a human being, he was so emaciated. I was heartbroken.

"Then one day I received word from the hospital that the baby would probably pass the crisis that day. I jumped into my car and drove down below Miami. I went off into a grove and got down behind a tree, burying my very forehead in the dirt, and cried unto God to be kind enough to restore my baby and not take it. I was overwhelmed with my unworthiness; I had forgotten God; I had neglected His service; I had given my whole thought to making money. Before I realized what I was doing, in place of praying for the baby, I was crying to God for myself. Then God spoke peace to my heart in His gracious tender forgiveness.

"I was so filled with joy that I jumped to my feet, got into the car, and rushed back to town. As I was driving along, I suddenly thought: 'Why, I haven't prayed for the baby at all!' Then came the assurance that in seeking God in His righteousness, I had pleased Him; and He would spare the baby.

"My wife met me at the door when I arrived at home. 'Oh,' she said, 'honey, I'm glad you're back. Word has just come from the hospital that the baby passed the crisis about thirty minutes ago and is going to get well!'

"I took her in my arms and said, 'Dear, I'm not surprised.'

195

Then I told her what had happened behind that tree between my heart and God.

"Finally I decided to move back to Alabama—and Doctor, what do you think I did? I did the same thing. Our baby was growing, he was healthy and strong and well; I had made a good deal of money; and I turned around and forgot God again. I found myself completely neglecting Him and His church and His service. Then came another crushing blow. While sitting in my office at my desk, I suddenly collapsed. I had known there was something wrong in my back for some time, but that day I became entirely helpless. They brought me to the hospital, and here I am. They tell me I'll never walk again, and I'm not surprised because I feel it's the hand of God, and I'm through now with all active work of any kind."

Dr. Forrest remonstrated: "Well, now, that's not necessarily so. I read in my Bible where God said, 'Let the wicked forsake his way, and the unrighteousness man his thoughts: and let him return [come back] unto the Lord.' And what'll He do about it? 'He will have mercy upon him; and . . . he will abundantly pardon.' The same God who forgave you for your neglect on one occasion is gracious and good enough to do it again. Let's pray about it."

Tears were trickling down the side of the invalid's face as he lay there on the pillow, absolutely helpless. Dr. Forrest knelt by the side of the bed, and the two prayed. The sick man reached around until he got hold of the preacher's hand and pressed it as Dr. Forrest prayed, meanwhile praying under his breath.

As Dr. Forrest rose from his knees, the invalid looked up with his face shining and his eyes bright. He said, "God has graciously heard your prayer; I feel that I'm back in my proper place with Him, but I'm still helpless."

"How come?" was the retort. "You may not be so helpless as you think if you're right with God. 'No good thing

196

will he withhold from them that walk uprightly.'" With these words Dr. Forrest left the man.

It was two days before he could get back to see him. When he opened the door to the room, he could see that an apparatus had been placed above the bed, whereby the patient could begin moving himself.

"Hallelujah," shouted the invalid, even before he could see Dr. Forrest. "Did they tell you the good news out there?"

"No, I haven't seen anybody, but I'm wondering how an old Methodist like you comes to shout like that."

"I heard you speak to somebody outside and recognized your voice. Didn't anybody tell you anything?"

"No."

"Why," he said, "they took an X-ray yesterday, and told me this morning that I was between third base and home. I'm going to get well. What do you know! I'm going to get well!"

He did recover, both physically and spiritually. Dr. Forrest corresponded with him for years; during all this time he stood right with God, walking in truth and righteousness and Christian service.

Of this incident Dr. Forrest concludes: "God is merciful and took his erring son back. Likewise He is more than willing to take back into His arms any sinning, but repentant, child of His."

Dr. Forrest had one experience in personal work that came as an answer to prayer for money, as well as being used of the Lord in the salvation of a man.

Some years ago, the school was facing a very acute need for several thousand dollars, and no one knew which way to turn to get it. Since the members of the Institute family have been accustomed all through the years to pray when in very pressing straits, that was one of the times when they were crying to God to put upon somebody's heart the desire to meet the need. Little did they know that the supply for that necessity was in the nearby town of Toccoa, Georgia.

In Toccoa lived a man whom Dr. Forrest had known for a number of years as just a street loafer. He was poorly dressed and always looked unshaven and really dirty in his personal appearance. As he was of a very good family, they were ashamed of the way he loafed around the streets; he was angry with them because they wouldn't take him into their homes. He lived in an old trailer, which was not only dirty and poorly kept, but even repulsive. It was no wonder the family felt as they did.

Dr. Forrest somehow was sorry for the fellow and took every opportunity to speak to him whenever he met him on the street. On several occasions he offered the fellow a little money to get something to eat, since he looked as though he might be hungry. The man never took the money, however, and always looked at Dr. Forrest in a peculiar kind of way when it was offered.

Finally, after a very serious conversation with Dr. Forrest about the Lord, the "bum" told him that he would accept the Lord Jesus Christ as his personal Saviour and that he would get off alone somewhere and pray about it, remembering the Scriptures that Dr. Forrest had given him. With this ray of hope, Dr. Forrest was more than ever encouraged to pray for the man's salvation.

The next thing that Dr. Forrest heard, to his shocked surprise, was that the man had suddenly dropped dead on the way home from a service of special meetings being held in town. Then this strange story was told.

This man who had looked so much like a bum had been a soldier in the First World War. When he collected his bonus checks at the end of the war, without saying anything to anybody about what he was doing (except a lawyer friend who attended to details for him), he bought up some humble negro homes around the edge of Toccoa and in neighboring towns. When he had bought as many as he had money for, he used the rent collected from these to buy others. At the time of his death, to the amazement of his family and friends, it was discovered from his lawyer friend that he had a great deal of property, most of it income-bearing.

He left a will. It was a strange document. It began with a preamble containing a eulogy of his friend, Dr. Forrest, telling how Dr. R. A. Forrest had spoken to him many times on the street, had prayed for him, and had finally won him to Christ. "Therefore," he said, "I do hereby will and bequeath all that I have, real and personal, to Dr. R. A. Forrest for the Toccoa Falls Institute and its works." He left one dollar to each of his brothers and one dollar to his sister.

By the time the will was probated and the property appraised, there was found to be something more than $16,000.00 in the estate—much more than the amount for which the Institute was praying at the time.

Then it was that Dr. Forrest discovered that the sister to whom only one dollar had been left was a widow and that she was having considerable trouble and was suffering real need. He did not then feel so happy about the whole matter and felt that he must do something for the widowed sister. In consequence, very much against the advice of his attorneys and friends, Dr. Forrest turned over half of the property to her. It was, of course, his privilege to do this, since the property had been willed to him for the Institute without restrictions of any kind. After doing this, he felt much better, knowing that the widow's sore need was supplied. With the balance he took care of the pressing debts of the Institute.

The Psalmist has declared: *He satisfieth the longing soul and filleth the hungry soul with goodness.* But the longing

199

soul cannot be satisfied until he becomes acquainted with the One who can satisfy. This requires witnessing. The Lord Jesus Christ told Simon Peter, and he in his epistle has passed the word on to His disciples: *Feed the flock of God which is among you.* The reward is sure: *And when the chief Shepherd shall appear, ye shall receive a crown of glory that fadeth not away.*

Dr. Forrest has always been a faithful witness—to small and great; surely a crown of glory is being made ready for him. Meanwhile, he shall continue to add stars to his crown as he comes in contact with his fellowmen.

Chapter Twenty-three

"For what is our hope, or joy, or crown of rejoicing? Are not even ye in the presence of our Lord Jesus Christ at his coming? For ye are our glory and joy."—I Thessalonians 2:19, 20

When a person looks back on a lifetime of labor, it is only natural for him to ask: "Has it been worthwhile? What profits have been gained? What dividends accrued?"

Dr. Forrest, too, has asked and answered these questions. In his inimitable style he summarizes: "We have discovered that there is no finer investment for life, energy, or money than in the development of living, breathing human beings. Through them, dividends will continue to accumulate until Jesus shall return, bringing His reward with Him, 'to give every man according as his work shall be.' Those who have, in any way, helped these young people in their preparation will surely share in the reward for the work they have helped to accomplish—whether they be workers at the school, contributors, or prayer warriors."

It is difficult to write about the dividends of Toccoa Falls, for there are so many. Which should be included? Scores of letters thrill the hearts of Dr. Forrest and his co-workers. As Dr. Forrest reads his mail, the phrases "How sweet!" "Isn't this lovely?" and "Praise the Lord!" are often repeated as he learns of new heights attained and new victories won by former students. Hundreds of testimonies praise the work of Toccoa Falls. Homecoming days are a paean of praise as hearts rejoice for what He has accomplished through His servants. Only a representative few may be presented here.

One does not have to leave Toccoa Falls to see dividends. Practically every person who comes as a student claims to be a Christian, but in many cases this only means he is a church member. Each year scores of students come to know Christ in a real and vital way; and many are called into definite, full-time service. One high school boy from Jacksonville, Florida, gave the following testimony: "I came to this school unsaved, but am now saved and rejoicing in the Lord. At Toccoa Falls Institute I was taught to believe on the Lord; so I can truthfully say that if it were not for this school I would still be in sin and unsaved." A girl from Illinois testifies: "TFI is my 'spiritual home,' for it was there in 1941 I found Christ and His salvation so full and free. I also praise Him for the courage and faith of His servants who claim His victory and strength in the face of difficulties." Similar statements are made by dozens of young people before the end of each school term.

The dividends extend from Toccoa Falls into Stephens and Habersham counties and into nearby towns, both in Georgia and South Carolina. The Bible College students cover approximately three thousand miles a month in order to reach about 2,500 children a week in services at schools, as well as an uncounted number of adults in street meetings, jail services, church services, visitation work, and other types of contacts. On one Sunday morning recently every pulpit in Stephens County was supplied by some one of the faculty or student body of Toccoa Falls Institute. Bare figures can never express the worth of these services—not till the harvest time can the full results be realized.

During the summer months the dividends reach into many portions of the United States, as students feel the challenge of full-time service. Much of the work accomplished has been in neglected places, where there is no possible chance of remuneration to help the young people through the next year of school. The students help in daily vacation Bible schools, tour in quartet work with staff representatives from the school, act as assistant pastors, work as counselors in Christian camps, and do many other types of Christian work.

Their testimonies are thrilling to read or hear, as can be told from the few included below:

"We praise the Lord for the 79 boys and girls who accepted Christ as their personal Saviour in our Bible schools in Alabama this summer. Boys and girls *want* to know the way of salvation. May the Lord help us who know Him to show them the way!"

"The past three months of presenting Christ to hungry hearts from an old gospel tent have brought untold blessing to our hearts as we have witnessed the working of God's wonderful grace in the lives of men!"

"During the summer I served as assistant pastor at a Methodist Church in Savannah, Georgia. Most of the month of August I was given complete charge. It was wonderful to be able to tell so many of the soul-saving power of our Lord and Saviour Jesus Christ and to put into practice that which God helped me to learn at Toccoa Falls Institute."

"We covered something like 3,500 miles, participating in 55 services in 52 days. We started with $10.00, a tank of gas, and a prayer meeting, not once asking anyone for money, food, or shelter, but making our needs known only to God. Not once did we stop for lack of funds, although several times we anxiously eyed the little treasury as it dwindled to a couple of dollars, and the contents of the gas tank as it sank to an alarming level, but God always slipped into the picture at the crucial moment to replenish our store."

Has it paid Dr. Forrest to put almost half a century of labor and sacrifice into the building of the Toccoa Falls Institute? The answer "yes" echoes and re-echoes through the entire world. The influence of this school has reached not only the area of its location, but to the four corners of the earth. The sun never sets on the activities of the alumni of Toccoa Falls.

During the Second World War, it was an inspiration to receive word from the young people in the armed forces, testifying that they were remaining true to the faith. One left school to enlist, that he might have opportunity to work among the Marines for Christ. His record continually showed that he was faithful in doing this. Another young man, one of ten chosen out of 1,200 naval cadets for advanced training, testified as to how he was given wisdom in answering the arguments of some ungodly boys. When one of them told him how foolish he was to accept Christ at full value, he replied: "When you give me something that will be better, I will accept that." The other cadets were silenced. Many boys, when released from service, came back to school, as one said, "more than glad to study."

Hundreds and hundreds of Christian workers in the United States are among the dividends from this school—and are now "laying up treasures in heaven."

A young man who had had very few privileges was accepted as a student at Toccoa Falls several years ago. Now a successful evangelist to the people of the Ozarks, he states:

"Heaven's door of opportunity came open when you, Dr. and Mrs. Forrest, gave this poor boy the privilege of entering that God-given institution. May God forever bless you and it."

One lad of humble means accepted the Lord at the age of sixteen and decided to enroll at Toccoa Falls. After overcoming many difficulties he entered the Institute.

"I came here without a cent and with a scanty wardrobe consisting for the most part of two 65¢ faded blue shirts and one pair of worn-out shoes. I had no hat, no coat, no full suit, no suitcase. It is remarkable to think how the Lord supplied my every need. I thank God for the hard places in my school work here—milking cows, washing dishes, doing farm work. Now I realize that those were the places that have prepared me for my ministry. Down by an old stump I spent hours in prayer to God, depending upon Him daily for my needs. It was here that I was rooted and grounded in the faith of Jesus Christ."

After completing his high school and college work, he went to Wheaton College for advanced work, and is now a successful pastor of a fine Christian and Missionary Alliance Church in a large city in Florida.

Extremely varied are the backgrounds of those who attend the Institute. Beginning with whatever education the student has acquired, the school workers, through God, lead him into a full and fruitful service. A number of years ago a boy from North Carolina enrolled in classes at Toccoa Falls. He had never known his parents, but was brought up by some old folks in his home community, much as a stray dog. Saved through a traveling preacher, he was taught enough so that he could read the Bible, although he couldn't read a newspaper. This awkward, gawky, and ignorant boy really loved the Lord. He used to go up into the hills behind the school buildings for "secret" prayer— but half a mile below on the campus he could be heard. Educated, he is now preaching the Word of God in North Carolina.

Not all students come from a distance, however. Local young people, too, have gone out from Toccoa Falls as emissaries for Christ. One of these, now a successful preacher in the Southern Presbyterian Church, began his training in public speaking at the age of nine. As master of ceremonies at the Institute-Community Christmas party, with excellent voice and poise he presented to the faculty

and Institute friends a number of mirth-provoking gifts. The
final gift was his master-stroke: since Dr. Forrest was a
preacher, the lad presented to him a live chicken. It is of
interest to note that Mrs. Forrest recognized the worth of
the lad—and went home from that party to kneel and dedi-
cate the boy to Christ for His service.

Dividends are reported in various ways. On one occasion
several former students, now active pastors, returned for a
visit after attending a Southern Baptist Convention held in
Atlanta. To hear their testimony as to how God is blessing
them in the work brought thrill after thrill. One young man
who is among the most successful told with tears in his eyes
that he could never forget the fact that had he not seen
Toccoa Falls Institute he would never have been engaged
in the work that is such a joy to him now. At the time of
the visit, he was pastor of the second largest rural Baptist
church in Virginia. Another was having a wonderful ministry as chaplain in a U. S. Army camp. A third was pastor
of a Baptist church with more than 1,200 members. He
came to Toccoa Falls as a married man to finish high school
and take the work of the Bible department. He worked
his way through school and supported his family, also.

Sometimes God has directed Dr. Forrest to accept as a
student a person to whom the doors of the school would
ordinarily be closed. Such was the case of George Akins,
a man who hitch-hiked from Savannah to Toccoa Falls. He
came without any recommendations, save a word from a
Presbyterian pastor, a friend of Dr. Forrest, stating that he
was sending this man to Toccoa Falls because he felt that
he should be given some Bible training and preparation.
Dr. Forrest was puzzled at first, as there was the stamp of
dissipation written all over the fellow's face.

Two or three nights after George's arrival, Dr. Forrest
started home from the campus. Although it was nearly
10:30, he had a strange feeling that he should go up to the

classrooms above the chapel. He had never gone up there at that time of night, but the conviction was so strong that, feeling there might be a fire, he went over. He climbed the steps and went from room to room, switching on the lights. When he came to the last room, he found George sobbing, with his face in his hands. Shocked and surprised to find anybody there, especially that late, Dr. Forrest went over, put his hand on the student's shoulder, and asked him to tell him the trouble. His answer was, "I'm going back to Savannah tomorrow."

"Why should you do that?"

"I'm not fit to be here in this kind of company. You don't know anything about me, do you?"

"No, but you told me that you're a born-again Christian, and that's all I want to know. If it will help you any to tell me about yourself, go ahead."

He then told Dr. Forrest that he had been a very dissipated man. He'd been brought up in a family where the older brothers drank a lot, and he had become a habitual drunkard at twenty-six when he was saved. Although ordinarily the school would not take a person like that, he was already a student. Dr. Forrest told him that surely he shouldn't go home. He talked and prayed with him until two o'clock in the morning.

The man stayed, memorized a great deal of Scripture, and often went to the woods to pray. One time he prayed concerning his financial needs. No one from his home town was interested in him, he was sick, and he was behind in his tuition. Discouraged, he went to his room, only to be called to Dr. Forrest's office. He was sure that he was being called in to be told he'd have to leave school if he couldn't pay his bill. But when he entered the office, Dr. Forrest told him that he'd been thinking a good deal about him, even in the morning when he first woke. He inquired as to how he was getting along. The young man poured out his troubles. Then Dr. Forrest looked him in the eye and said, "Today some money came to me from up North, and it was stated I was to give it to somebody that I thought was worthy and needed it. God has laid it on my heart to apply it to your account." Tearful, George left the office, assured of the fact that God hears and answers prayer.

After two years at Toccoa Falls, this man went back to Savannah. There he started a rescue mission. At first it was in a little dilapidated place, but God continued to answer prayer. Now the mission has its quarters in a $40,000.00 building. The men of affairs in Savannah believe in him and his work; the ministers and the business men support him. Hundreds of unfortunate men have found a haven in his mission. Later he also established a mission camp for children and young people, where thousands have given their hearts to God. He also has a small Christian high school.

George Akins has testified: "It's good to be a Christian. It's good to know that back in 1933 God saved me and led me to Toccoa Falls Bible Institute. TFI is home to me—it's where I learned to pray, to memorize Scripture, and to preach. Dr. and Mrs. Forrest, Mr. and Mrs. Barnes, and all the others of those days will never know what their lives have meant to me until they get on the other side. I thank God for that day when Dr. Forrest called me into the office and had the good word that somebody had paid my tuition."

The young man who came to Toccoa Falls with the marks of dissipation written all over his face, thinking he was not worthy to associate with folks he met there has now developed into a prince and a man of God, doing a wonderful work, showing that the grace of God that bringeth salvation is able to change a man and use him who otherwise would be useless.

Several of the graduates of Toccoa Falls have emulated

Dr. Forrest in the founding of schools of their own. Most of these are on the foreign field, where they become "little TFI's." In the States there is one school organized by a graduate who had to wait three years to enter the Institute —because he was too young.

This lad accepted Christ when he was thirteen. Out of curiosity he decided to attend a tent meeting being held in his town and rode his bicycle to the place where the tent was pitched. Before he left the meeting that night, he had become "a new creature in Christ Jesus." As he started for home, his bicycle was forgotten, for his heart was full of praises to God for the new joy that had come into his life. It was only after he had gone about half a mile that he remembered that he had ridden to the service.

Three years later the boy, Bill Watson, entered the Institute, brought down by his Sunday-school teacher, Janie Hargraves. After his graduation he was invited by Dr. Forrest, as District Superintendent of the Alliance, to engage in tent work in Florida. Bill pitched a big ragged tent in St. Petersburg and had wonderful meetings. That ragged tent later became the St. Petersburg Gospel Tabernacle.

Later Bill, in a modest quiet way, started a Bible school. When the Florida boom of the late twenties burst, Bill was able to buy the Temple Terrace property at a price far below its value. That was the starting of the Florida Bible Institute. Afterwards this property was sold at a huge profit and the school moved to a beautiful place in Clearwater, where it still functions to the glory of God as Trinity Bible College.

This aside will be of interest—and will help prove that the dividends may exceed our comprehension: at Billy Graham's outdoor meeting in Washington, D. C., he asked Dr. Forrest to sit on the platform and to offer prayer. After the meeting some of Dr. Forrest's friends gathered round him and were chatting. One man said, "This is so wonderful, seeing this great crowd of people assembled to hear Billy Graham, but isn't it true that he really got his vision for this kind of work while down at a Bible School in Clearwater, Florida, conducted by a fellow named Bill Watson?"

Dr. Forrest answered, "So I understand."

Someone else spoke up and said, "Isn't it true that Bill Watson got his vision for what he did from Toccoa Falls?"

"Yes, sir. He was one of our students in the early days."

They stood for a long time talking about the manner in which events could be traced farther back—Janie Hargraves would get a slice of reward for sending Bill Watson to Toccoa Falls, the Institute would get some for preparing Bill and sending him to Clearwater, and so on. It's the multiplication which is experienced in this kind of work that makes it so valuable.

It is wonderful to receive "tidings from afar"—to hear of dividends around the world. From our next-door neighbor, Cuba, come heart-warming reports, both from missionaries sent there from the United States and from former Cuban students at Toccoa Falls.

While a fine young lady, a zealous Christian worker, was attending Toccoa Falls, a young man visited the school and spoke about mission work in Cuba. Later these two married and together went through the heart-breaking pioneer period of the work in Cuba, eventually establishing a strong mission under the direction of the Free Will Baptist Foreign Mission Board. Recently they wrote thus of their work:

> "We have just returned from one of our newest fields with our hearts thrilled with what we saw in this, one of the most neglected spots of Cuba. The roads were almost impassable. Eight of us with a heavy rope had to pull the Ford up out of mud sink holes. When we went into this village we were received with open arms.

We met fine converted men who had walked great distances in the rain to attend the services. Their faces glowed with divine love. We thank God we could leave a young man to minister there."

A few years ago Dr. and Mrs. Forrest went to Havana, Cuba, visiting some of the former Institute students who are now in full-time Christian service there. One of these, in addition to pastoring the First Presbyterian Church of Havana, has established and directs a Chinese church gathered out of the more than 25,000 Chinese who live in that area. Another former student is now Moderator of the Havana Presbytery. And so the dividends in this island accrue.

From the earliest days of the Institute, mission work has been emphasized. The first two missionaries who left Toccoa Falls were the Misses Mary Spooner and Annie E. Thomas, who felt the call to Central America. A short while later Miss Annie Erickson sailed for South America, Miss Carolyn Warner for China, and Miss Elizabeth Kennedy for French West Africa. By 1920 Toccoa Falls was being represented on several continents.

In 1914, John M. Turner of Royston, Georgia, started to India by way of Toccoa Falls. He later went as an independent missionary to Calcutta, then back into the interior to the Ganges river. On his round-the-world trip in 1936, Dr. Forrest visited Rev. Turner at Benares, India. The way the natives bowed and scraped before Jack Turner was evidence to Dr. Forrest as to how he is succeeding. After twenty years in India and at the age of sixty-three, Rev. Turner plans to go back for one more term.

Rev. and Mrs. Frank Reifsnyder are two early graduates of Toccoa Falls who have given their lives in His service. For many years they have labored in South America, serving among the wild Indian tribes on the eastern side of the

211

Andes Mountains. They established a trading post for the savage Campa Indians at the head waters of the Amazon River. When the Indians came to trade, Rev. Reifsnyder got acquainted with them and learned their language. Whereas anybody else who tried to penetrate into their territory would probably get a poisoned arrow between his shoulders, Rev. Reifsnyder has gained their utmost confidence and affection and is perfectly free to go anywhere he pleases. On one trip out among the Indians, he contracted tropical fever. The Indians made a makeshift stretcher and carried him on their shoulders many miles back to his station. He is such a friend to the Campas and has done so much constructive work to help them that he has been decorated by the Peruvian Government for these services, and is looked upon by the governmental officials as an authority on Peruvian Indian affairs.

It is always a time of rejoicing when former students return to the campus and tell of the victories they've won for Christ. Their presence and reports also lend an incentive to the students toward more earnest prayer, more sacrificial giving, and more sincere effort in preparing themselves to follow in His footsteps—even to the ends of the earth. Praise God! The challenge given them of the millions in darkness is being met. While the early graduates remain true, even to the death, more and more within the past fifteen years have laborers from Toccoa Falls been thrust forth into the "harvest field." In the early months of 1950, for example, nine graduates from the Institute left for various mission fields—four to Costa Rica, one to Japan, two to Anglo-Egyptian Sudan, and two to French West Africa.

One can easily understand the joy that floods Dr. Forrest's heart as he sees these young people join the forces that have gone to the "regions beyond" to tell the message of the cross to those who have never heard. What a thrill he gets in reading reports from them like the excerpts included here.

French West Africa: "The farther we get away from TFI, the more we realize the value of the training we received there. God has been good to us to allow us to come under the influence of the godly men and women who make up the faculty and administrative staff of Toccoa Falls. When I first came there I was so green and proud, and it took a lot of cultivating, pruning and tender care (and I might add patience) to get me to the place where I would be capable of bearing a little fruit; I praise the Lord for His blessings."

Anglo-Egyptian Sudan, East Africa: "Several boys from the villages come to us to learn to read and we feel very much encouraged. These are Christian boys, and we feel there is a softening of hearts to the Lord Jesus. Recently, one young Dinka told me, 'Chief, don't become tired of us and leave us. The Dinkas are a black-hearted people, but they will one day come to love the things of God.'"

British Cameroons, Africa: "With a heart full of thanksgiving to you and the school for all that you did for me, let me turn back as did the leper of old, and thank God for you—then thank you for letting Him use you in training young men to go forth into the great harvest fields. As I go forth into the work in this land, may I work as you have taught me so that many, many may come to know and accept Christ as their way of salvation."

College Senior from Canada, leaving for Africa: "I shall always be grateful for the training TFI has offered in preparation for my life's work. Now it is with joy that I set my face toward missionary service in Africa. It is not a sacrifice: it is a real privilege to look forward to witnessing for my Saviour in Africa."

Akola, Berar, India: "Our hearts were thrilled only a month ago when hundreds of seeking souls attended our annual camp meeting. They came from far and near, by train, bus, bullock cart, or on foot to this spiritual feast for six days. Many who had come heavy hearted met the Lord in a very real way and left with peace of heart and assurance of salvation. Many of these people returned to villages where no other Christians live, and where they hear the Gospel only about once a year. Can you blame us for praying for new missionaries? We are grateful for Toccoa Falls Institute as a 'Recruiting Station.'"

Costa Rica, Central America: "Yesterday the conference at Chira ended and it was such a blessing. I have never been in a place where everyone seemed so happy in the Lord. The whole three days I never heard a cross word. There were some professions of faith, and many came to hear the Gospel who had before laughed and scoffed at the missionaries."

Managua, Nicaragua: "This is a 'Call to Prayer' from the field which has become the Central American Mission's greatest challenge—Nicaragua. Together with the areas of Managua, Granada, Carazo and Rivas, where the work is better cared for, the total number of souls to which we are responsible to preach the Gospel is no less than 600,000! Our missionary force consists of one single lady nearly ready for retirement, one single man whose furlough is due in six months, and ourselves, the only couple. Will you cry unto God that He will send forth His chosen ones to Nicaragua, to 'possess the land'? We feel that a new day is dawning for this land, a day of revival and great spiritual out-pouring."

French West Africa: "We are rejoicing in the way the Lord has worked during the past year. In looking over our report we found that there were 616 who have accepted Christ as their Saviour, and 84 who have taken the important step of baptism."

As flashes of lightning briefly rend the darkness, so do these few sketches and testimonies endeavor to give a momentary glance into the dividends of Toccoa Falls Institute. What better investment of lives, prayers, or money

214

could be made? In what other kind of enterprise is there better security, sounder purpose, or finer dividends? Is it any wonder that Dr. Forrest often says: "If I had my life to live over again, I would make the same decisions and do the same things that I have done—except that I'd try to do them better."

Chapter Twenty-four

"Thou, O God, hast proved us: thou hast tried us, as silver is tried. We went through fire and through water: but thou broughtest us out into a wealthy place."—PSALM 66:10, 12b

WHILE DR. FORREST, in 1913, sat on a rock near the smoking embers of Haddock Inn, weeping over his vanished hopes and dreams, the Lord drew near unto him. "Weep not," He comforted, "thou shalt have beauty for ashes. Dost thou not know: this school is the planting of the Lord; it shall continue."

During the past forty-five years God has abundantly proved His promise. Time and time again He has carried the school through vicissitudes—through fires, depression, two world wars, and other emergencies. He has tried the school, "as silver is tried," and He has brought it out "into a wealthy place." Hundreds of fine young people have had life and character transformed while being educated, and graduates are now to be found throughout the world in fruitful service to God and humanity. The physical assets have grown from 100 acres to 1,085 acres of land, and the buildings from the one hotel to more than sixty buildings. The value of the property has increased from the original $25,000.00 to more than $1,000,000.00. From the beginning it has been evident that the school is a miracle of God's provision and care.

"It has been forty years of miracles," Dr. Forrest told a vast audience of friends, students, parents, and alumni during the Commencement season of 1951.

216

It is true that the Toccoa Falls Institute has been a testimony of God's faithfulness from the day Dr. Forrest made a down payment of ten dollars on the original hotel building right down to the present moment. But what of the future? Many organizations and institutions, founded nobly and carried on wisely, have lost their purpose and their vision when the founder is obliged to pass on the reins of administration to others. What of the Toccoa Falls Institute? During the many years of its existence, one man has largely been responsible for the direction of its affairs. Has provision been made in event of his promotion to higher service?

There is no doubt that the same miracle-working God will provide in the future just as He has in the past; and Dr. Forrest, confident that He "which hath begun a good work . . . will perform it until the day of Jesus Christ," has recently led the other members of the administration in taking steps to insure the future of the Institute. It was with rejoicing that the following article was published in the "Toccoa Falls News" of June, 1955, announcing these steps:

"Since the founding of Toccoa Falls Institute in 1911 the heavy responsibility of its direction and growth has rested largely upon the shoulders of Dr. R. A. Forrest and a very small number of men associated with him. The vision, faith, and sacrifice of Dr. Forrest has laid a great foundation for this institution. For more than twenty-five years the Rev. E. Kelly Barnes, after receiving his training at Toccoa Falls and Wheaton College, has labored as superintendent of the school as he has given leadership to a wonderful staff and faculty.

"Dr. Forrest and Mr. Barnes, having carried so much of the burden of responsibility and leadership for the Institute for forty-four years, felt that the time had come to enlarge the organization of the school so that a broader base would be established for the future growth and ministry of Toccoa Falls Institute. After much thought, discussion, and prayer, a new Constitution was approved by the Executive Committee; and a Board of Trustees consisting of twenty-one men was selected.

"On April 12, 1955, most of the newly elected trustees gathered at Toccoa Falls, and on hearing the Constitution read they heartily agreed to its clear statement of faith in the revealed truths of historic, Biblical Christianity and to the stated purpose of the school. All of these splendid Christian men agreed to serve as trustees of the school and to perpetuate and extend its wonderful ministry in the years to come.

"The trustees were carefully chosen because of their firm belief in our doctrinal statement and for their representation of various callings and geographical sections of our country. Industrialists, business men, pastors, attorneys, and alumni are all represented on the board.

"The trustees elected the following to serve as officers of the school for a three-year term: Dr. R. A. Forrest, President; Dr. J. A. Bandy, Vice-President; Rev. Troy Damron, Secretary-Treasurer; and Rev. E. Kelly Barnes, Superintendent. These men, plus three others, comprise the Executive Committee, which between the annual meetings of the Board of Trustees will direct the affairs of the school in keeping with the policy determined by the trustees. (Mrs. R. A. Forrest was elected Honorary Secretary of the Executive Committee, in recognition of her many years of service as active secretary of this committee.)

"This enlarged organization with such a splendid board of trustees assures the whole body of Christian faith that Toccoa Falls Institute will continue to maintain its original purpose and testimony so solidly established by the life and ministry of its founder, Dr. R. A. Forrest. It also gives assurance that the school will enlarge its great ministry under the energy and wise guidance of such an able board of Christian men."

In this same meeting the Board of Trustees unanimously voted on the following resolution:

"Recognizing that the great accomplishments, the physical assets, the sound spiritual emphasis, and the solid training which has prepared young people who are creditably serving the Lord in many responsible positions of trust throughout the world are largely due to the vision—faith—sacrifice—and consecrated lives of Dr. and Mrs. R. A. Forrest—therefore, be it resolved by a standing vote we record our deep appreciation for these faithful servants of God."

"First, survival; then expansion; and last, approval." As Dr. Forrest looks back over the years, he mentally reviews the vales of vicissitudes and the summits of success which marked the fight for survival and the years of expansion. Thank God, the shadows of the valleys have always been swallowed up in the joys of the heights.

"Last, approval." Approval has been given by God in the many miracles with which He has blessed the school. Approval has also been shown in the supply, by means of gifts of consecrated Christians, of funds necessary to carry on the work. In speaking of the present finances of the Institute, Dr. Forrest says: "In view of the fact that we do not have any church or society who carries any responsibility for our finances, we are profoundly grateful to God for His mercy and goodness, and for the many miracles He has performed to keep the school going. He has again and again demonstrated His pleasure in the work, and our confidence is in Him. We thank the many friends who continually evidence their confidence in the school by sending contributions. Only recently we were again overwhelmed by two separate gifts of $10,000.00 each; but we are just

219

as thankful for the 'widow's mite.' God will use both to further His work."

Dr. Forrest has always been characterized by his zeal and energy in pushing forward. Even now he dreams of the improvements he should like to see made on the campus.

"For the school to function at its best," he says, "we need three more buildings. It would be fine to have a chapel large enough to accommodate the entire student body and some guests. This chapel would be used for religious services only.

"The second building is a dormitory for young men comparable to LeTourneau Hall for young ladies. While there is actually enough room to accommodate the present number of students, the boys' dormitories are frame buildings, remodeled from buildings originally used for other purposes, and are showing the effects of age.

"The third building is a 'must' and should probably take precedence over the two just mentioned. It is a new library. Plans for such a building have been drawn by a consecrated and efficient architect; the cost would be around $90,000.00. There are approximately 16,000 books in the present library (the original dining room), and the room is so small that many of these books are simply stacked up in great piles and therefore are not always available to the students. It is the purpose of the administration to have the money in hand for the building before it is started. Several thousand dollars have already been pledged for such a building. What a privilege it would be for someone who can to erect such a building as a memorial!"

Were the Toccoa Falls Institute not "the planting of the Lord," there would be no use in planning its continuation. Thank God—it is "His doing." Toccoa Falls Institute is more than buildings joined together on rugged hillsides. It is a dream of service and of worship and of praise come

220

true in a picturesque setting—in the beautiful hills of north Georgia with their gorgeous foliage and flowers, the birds singing and squirrels scampering about. Through and over all the material things there is ever a warm, rich, wholesome spiritual atmosphere. Strangers coming on the campus often comment that "the atmosphere feels different here. We noticed it as soon as we turned off the highway. What causes it?" The ground is holy ground, dedicated to the glory of and service for God. The love of God permeates every corner. The purpose of the school is ever apparent. Former students turn their footsteps back to its campus whenever possible—for refreshing—and beseech the prayers of its people for their lives and work.

"Among other reasons for the existence of Toccoa Falls Institute," summarizes Dr. Forrest, "is the fact that while it is the oldest Bible school south of the Mason-Dixon Line, it is one of the few Bible schools of which we know where the adult student has the opportunity not only for the Bible course, but also a fully accredited high school course preparing him for the Bible college work; all the while holding forth the most important thing—which is the development of Christian character and life. Surely the world needs leaders of this kind, and we are trying our best to produce them. The record of the past forty-five years is studded many times with rare jewels and we are hoping to produce many more of them until Jesus comes to gather His gems 'from every kindred, tongue, and tribe.'"

Epilogue

"I have fought a good fight, . . . I have kept the faith: Henceforth there is laid up for me a crown of righteousness, which the Lord, the righteous judge, shall give me at that day: and not to me only, but unto all them also that love his appearing."—II TIMOTHY 4:7, 8

ON THE EVENING OF November 23, 1898, two boys knelt side by side in a little cottage prayer meeting. They were best friends; they were inseparable; they planned to go into partnership in business, build houses side by side, and even marry sisters—if they could find two who would have them.

The decisions those teen-age boys made that night changed all the plans and altered the courses of their lives. One lad, Richard Forrest, rose from his knees "a new creature in Christ Jesus." The other deliberately rejected Christ.

A few years ago Dr. Forrest, without really knowing why, stopped for a few hours in his old home town. He met a friend who said, "I know what brought you here. You've come to the funeral of your old boyhood friend."

"Is he dead?" asked Dr. Forrest. "How did he die?"

"I'm ashamed to tell you, but he died of delirium tremens. He was a drunkard for many years."

* * * * * * * * *

We pause, before closing the pages of this book, to pay honor to the man who, as a youth, made the right decision

222

and who, by the grace of God, pressed forward in unselfish, untiring service for Him.

Many honors have been bestowed upon this man after God's own heart. He served as Chaplain of the Georgia Senate during the session of 1945-46. In 1949 he was selected "Man of the Year" in both Stephens County and the city of Toccoa, Georgia. He was presented the key to the city of Charlotte, North Carolina, while addressing a group of business men there in 1951. He has been mentioned in *Who's Who in America;* and he was recognized by a two-page write-up, plus a full-page portrait, in W. G. Cooper's Biographical Volume of *The Story of Georgia,* published in 1938. He numbers among his friends many of national and international fame, in both religious and secular circles.

He is dearly loved by the common folk. One dear old soul told him she liked his preaching "because you're so simple, like us folks."

He has been a tremendous blessing and inspiration to countless numbers of people around the world, both directly and through the students sent out from the school of his founding.

The feeling of the students toward him is aptly summarized by the testimony of one young man who traveled with him one summer: "I was just like every other Christian, and in traveling with him and seeing his consistency, the sweetness of his life, his regular punctuality, and everything about his life—that has meant everything to me down through the years. I would never try to preach like him— I don't think anyone could—but his regular consistent everyday Christian life and wonderful messages have always been a great blessing and inspiration to my life."

This, then, is the man, a man after God's own heart, a sweet and noble Christian character—Dr. R. A. Forrest. He needs no monument: the Toccoa Falls Institute is far more impressive and enduring than any memorial made of stone. Furthermore, those who have carried and will carry the beliefs and traditions of the Toccoa Falls Institute across this land and into far countries *as lively stones, are built up a spiritual house, an holy priesthood, to offer up spiritual sacrifices, acceptable to God by Jesus Christ.* Their deeds, too, will constitute a living memorial, keeping alive the vision of Dr. Forrest and his beloved wife.

As long as time shall last, many will turn their thoughts to days spent at the Toccoa Falls Institute, will thank the Lord for the vision and the consecrated lives of the Forrests, and will praise Him for accomplishments attained through the lessons learned in "that beautiful spot of the Creation for which our great God seems to have had special care"-- the Toccoa Falls Institute.

Praise God for a man whose ear was so attuned to the Lord that he could hear His command, whose heart never failed as he set forth to carry out His desires, and whose vision has not grown dim through the passing years as he has put His plans into fruition—the man Dr. R. A. Forrest.